GEOGRAPHY THROUGH ART

U.S. & International Art Projects for Kids!

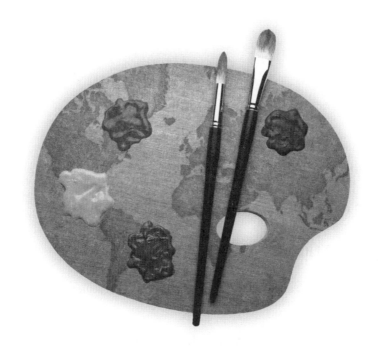

BY SHARON JEFFUS & JAMIE ARAMINI

Geography Through Art by Sharon Jeffus and Jamie Aramini

Copyright 2008, 2012 Geography Matters, Inc.

Published by Geography Matters, Inc.

Previously published by Visual Manna as *Teaching Geography Through Art*, copyright 2001. *Geography Through Art* published by Geography Matters, Inc. is fully revised and rewritten.

ISBN: 978-1-931397-58-2
Library of Congress Control Number: 2008923054

Printed in the United States of America

Geography Matters
800-426-4650
www.geomatters.com

DEDICATION

I would like to dedicate my work on this book to my wonderful father who went to be with the Lord on December 26, 2000. This book is for him. He was going to write a book for me on succeeding in business from his experience. Although this book is about geography, I want to give him the credit for my love of learning and ability to write.

~Sharon Jeffus

I would like to dedicate my work on this book to all the favorite children in my life: Nick & Alyssa Aramini; Jacob Childers; Darrell, Bobby, & Abby Johnson; Taylor Jones; Zack Lose; Maggie & Megan Miller; Katie Nichols, and my favorite of favorites—Joey Aramini. You all are my inspiration for writing something that is fun.

~Jamie Aramini

ACKNOWLEDGEMENTS

We wish to extend our heartfelt appreciation to Kathy Wright who drew many of the illustrations in this book. Her tireless efforts to create QuickSketch examples to help students draw was a tremendous contribution to *Geography Through Art*.

Thanks to Josh Wiggers for creating the wonderful maps; to Cindy Wiggers for providing the geography information that introduces each continent; to Alex Wiggers for the beautiful new cover design and layout.

About the Authors

Sharon Jeffus

Sharon Jeffus has a B.S.S.E. in Art Education from John Brown University and earned her certification to teach English from the University of Arkansas. She studied painting at Metropolitan in Denver and sculpting at Southern Illinois University.

Sharon taught in the public schools for ten years in Arkansas, Oklahoma, and Missouri. She taught Intensive English as an adjunct lecturer at the University of Missouri-Rolla; has given presentations on teaching art to college classes at Azusa Pacific University and Columbia College; taught in a Christian school in Branson, Missouri; and has given presentations to the Associated Christian Schools International Conventions across America.

She left the public school system to write books, travel, and homeschool her two sons. She has written over twenty books and owns the internationally known company Visual Manna which she founded with her late husband Richard. Sharon developed the Visual Manna teaching method where art is integrated with art appreciation, techniques, vocabulary, and core subjects. She is a regular writer for The Old Schoolhouse magazine and has written for a number of other educational resources. She has authored an Indian Arts and Crafts program that was rated outstanding by the Bureau of Indian Affairs, and her materials are recommended by Montessori.

Jamie Aramini

Jamie Aramini is the author of *Eat Your Way Around the World*, *Geography Through Art* with Sharon Jeffus, and the *Adventures of Munford* series. She graduated co-valedictorian of her high school class and was a Kentucky Governor's Scholar. She is currently raising her two sons, a flock of chickens, and a miniature Schnauzer named Sophie. Her hobbies include organic gardening, cooking, and teaching writing at her local homeschool co-op.

Visit www.jamiearamini.com to learn more about Jamie.

TABLE OF CONTENTS

INTRODUCTION

From the Authors

Dear Reader,

Thank you for purchasing *Geography Through Art*. We hope you will use it to supplement your geography or history curriculum or as a basis for teaching art.

Why art? What is it about art that makes it such a valuable learning tool? Why waste your time drawing the Eiffel Tower when you can just read about it in a book? The answer is simple: Hands-on activities reinforce knowledge in a concrete way. An art project can turn an otherwise uninspiring subject into something exciting and challenging! Combining art with geography adds deeper understanding of the peoples of the world and how they live.

Geography Through Art was first published in 2001 by Visual Manna. This rewritten and revised version, published by Geography Matters, has several added features to enhance your use of the book. Be sure to familiarize yourself with these special features described in the instructions.

This book includes more than 100 art projects touching on 27 countries in six continents. After you have completed the world section, it is not necessary do the rest of the projects in order. So feel free to select activities by region, country, or topic. The directions for each project serve only as a guide to get you started. Never let your students feel limited by what the book says! If, for example, they are supposed to draw a picture of the Great Pyramids, and they would rather build it in the back yard out of rocks, let them do that instead. Help them to develop their own creativity and think outside of the box. Then they will have an original work of art that they can truly be proud of.

A parting thought to share with your budding artists: *Never* compare your work to someone else's. We each have our own skills and talents. There is no right or wrong in art. Just use your imagination and do your best!

We hope that you and your students enjoy the projects. You will not only learn about geography, but also about the cultures and lifestyles of countries all over the world.

Sharon Jeffus & Jamie Aramini

Note: Please tell us about your experience using this book. Email the publisher at gta@geomatters.com with your questions, comments, or completed art projects. Thanks!

INSTRUCTIONS

Geography Through Art has a number of interesting features to enhance student appreciation of art and impact student understanding of its connectedness to the world in which we live. These features are highlighted by special boxes, icons, or font-type.

QUICKSKETCH

QuickSketch inserts provide students with the opportunity to practice sketching. Using the picture as a reference they can draw the topic listed. Remind students to label their sketch with the country, title, and date and place it in their geography notebook. (More about the geography notebook in the next section.)

Artist Profile

Profiles of famous artists and famous works of art contain many interesting tidbits of information. They are also a great starting point for a research paper or project.

Culture Connection

Take special note of the boxes labeled "Culture Connection." These will help students understand how different cultures relate to each other. What things do they have in common? What things are different? As you go through the projects in the book, help them try to think of other culture connections we might have missed.

Internet Resources

When you see the WebLink icon, it indicates that we have identified useful websites that will enhance your study. Geography Matters hosts a page on its website designed especially for users of *Geography Through Art* where you'll find live links to these sites. Simply sign up at www.geomatters.com/GTA to access this free information.

Country Menus

When you see the FoodLink icon, you'll find recipes to prepare a meal from this country in *Eat Your Way Around the World* by Jamie Aramini.

Difficulty Level

This book is designed to be used with different age levels. Projects are labeled with stars based on the difficulty level. Projects with no stars are appropriate for all ages.

Primary ☆   Intermediate ☆☆   Secondary ☆☆☆

Primary or Intermediate projects are also suitable for older students. Many can be adapted to a younger level by simply providing more help from an adult, especially when using scissors or other sharp objects.

Glossary

Art terms in bold are defined in the glossary and can be added to any vocabulary study.

GEOGRAPHY NOTEBOOK

Studying geography is interesting, especially when coupling it with another subject. You might expect to see a history course linked with geography but art and geography? Yes! It's a natural. In fact, it is easy to integrate geography into nearly any subject of study including science, literature, and current events.

To connect geography with the art lessons we've included a brief overview of each continent in the beginning of each section. In addition basic continent map are provided to aid students in identifying where the art projects originate and to locate places mentioned in the geography summaries. When you have selected a project, ask the student to find that country on the map. Take note also what countries or bodies of water surround the country in focus.

We highly recommend students create their own personal geography notebook. Three-ring binders work well for this. Divide tabbed sections according to continent and place completed drawings, paintings, maps, reports, and more in the appropriate sections. Some projects will not fit in the binder, but can still be included by taking a picture of the project and putting it in the notebook. Students will be reminded to add to their notebooks periodically. Reproducible outline maps, Countries of the World Fact Sheet, and Illustrated Geography Terms sheets, found in the Appendix, are all interesting inclusions for the geography notebook.

Maps

Outline maps of each continent are located in the Appendix. Feel free to copy the maps for your study. Have students use the outline maps to label countries, capitals, and bodies of water. They can also shade and label other physical features. Be sure to provide students with a good classroom atlas appropriate to their level. See Recommendations at the end of this section for suggested atlases.

This book is packed full of projects, so just have a good time with your students. Some students will especially enjoy maps and geography. There are a number of other mapping activities and helpful hints to guide your student in getting the most out of the geography study.

Mapping Ideas

• Open the atlas and have your students locate the countries for themselves.

• Have students label countries and their capitals on the continent outline map.

• Label bodies of water.

• Using the atlas for reference, see what the climate is like in the region. Compare to your own climate. Shade a fresh copy of the map to show climate.

• Color in the countries on the continent outline map. Cover the sheet with contact paper. Cut along country boundaries. Now you have a puzzle. Store puzzle pieces in a sheet protector and place in the geography notebook.

• Draw and label major rivers and other interesting physical features.

• Place an "x" or triangle at the highest point in the continent (or country).

Helpful Hints

- Place names can have different spellings from atlas to atlas.

- Neater students may prefer to label their places lightly in pencil and then go over it with a fine-tipped marker when they are satisfied with the look of their map.

- Obtain outline maps of countries. These will have larger scale to label.

- If you are covering the material in one continent at a time, give students an outline map at the close of the study and see how many countries they can label from memory. See what else they can label.

- Place all outline map projects in the appropriate continent section of the geography notebook.

Countries of the World Fact Sheet

For further study, copy the Countries of the World fact sheet from the Appendix and let your students research the information. Most of the data can be found in an atlas, encyclopedia, Internet (worldatlas.com), or an almanac. Have students draw the country's flag, or place a picture of the flag in the space provided. Use the additional space for other pictures, student drawings, or information that students have learned. (A sample of China is included.) This page can be added to the geography notebook or can be placed in its own report folder to create a Countries of the World student notebook.

Illustrated Geography Terms

Copy the Illustrated Geography Terms template for students to sketch physical features of the earth. Lines are provided to write a brief definition from the geography terms glossary. Students can add more terms as they are learned. (A sample sheet is included.) Make a separate tabbed section in the geography notebook for these pages.

Recommendations

Each of these resources are available from Geography Matters. See page 192 for ordering information.

- *Beginner World Atlas.* Student atlas for kindergarten through third graders.

- *Intermediate World Atlas.* Atlas for students in fourth grade through eighth grade.

- *Answer Atlas.* Atlas for adult reference or high school students.

- World Almanac. Reference for completing the Countries of the World project.

- Geography Terms Chart. Labeled drawing of various physical features; a great visual reference to help students draw physical features when doing the Illustrated Geography Terms project.

- *The Ultimate Geography and Timeline Guide* by Maggie Hogan and Cindy Wiggers. Contains detailed information on how to teach geography, creating notebooks, using timelines, reproducible timeline figures, and more; also includes in-depth unit studies on the continents for middle school and high school students.

- *Uncle Josh's Outline Map Book* (or CD ROM) by George and Hannah Wiggers. For students who really enjoy using maps; provides a plethora of simple reproducible outline maps for any topic of study.

ART TIPS

In this section, you will find basic information on using the color wheel and guidelines and tips to share with your students when using different art mediums. Feel free to suggest students change mediums for a project if desired. For example, if students really enjoyed drawing an object, let them paint it in watercolor or use oil pastels with the same subject.

Using the Color Wheel

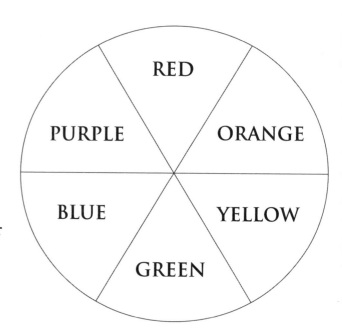

- Before starting any work of art, it is helpful to know about the color wheel. This will aid you in selecting the colors for your work. Look at the color wheel on this page as you read over this information. Keep the following things in mind as you choose the colors for each of your assignments:

- The primary colors are red, yellow, and blue.

- The secondary colors are green, orange, and purple. When mixing paints, you can create the secondary colors by mixing the primary colors next to them. For example, mixing red and blue make purple.

- Complementary colors are colors opposite each other on the color wheel. Using complementary colors together creates a bold statement. For example, purple against yellow will really stand out.

- When mixing paints, do not add black to darken your color. Add the color's complement. For example, to make a darker red, use green.

- Warm colors are red, orange, and yellow. These colors really stand out in a piece of art and make it more exciting.

- Cool colors are blue, purple, and green. These colors blend in well and calm down the tone of your art.

Drawing

Students are often hesitant to draw a picture of an object. They may lack the knowledge and confidence to succeed at such an endeavor. While some people may instinctively be able to draw a realistic figure, for most people it is a learned art. The only way to learn is to practice! Here are some tips to guide your students in their sketches.

- Resting your hand on your drawing can lead to unattractive smears and smudges. Use a scrap piece of paper under your hand to protect your art.

- What do the letters and numbers on a pencil mean? H means hard, and B means black. The harder the pencil, the less color will be transferred to the paper. The softer the pencil, the more color, the darker the line. If you have a wide range of sketching pencils, experiment to see which is best fit for your piece. A pencil marked B or 2B is a good choice for a basic sketch.

- A good choice for an eraser is a "kneadable" one. Other erasers may damage your paper or simply move your pencil marks around. A "kneadable" eraser can be kneaded after each use to ensure that it will be clean the next time you erase. By using it, the pencil marks stay on the eraser and aren't transferred back to your paper.

- Always keep your pencils sharp.

- Always start out with very light pencil marks. Progressively work up to darker marks.

- Begin each drawing with the basic shapes that create the outline of your object. Use squares, circles, ovals, and triangles. Then add more and more detail, erasing extra lines as needed.

- In a landscape, things in the foreground (the front) of a picture are darker, clearer, and larger. In the background, objects become less detailed, less colorful, and smaller.

- Pay close attention to real-life objects. Use shading to show where a shadow would normally appear.

- Practice using texture in your sketches. Sketch artists use many patterns to add variety and depth to a picture. Try using straight lines, dots, or squiggles.

- Make a line darker by pressing harder on the page. (Don't press so hard that you damage the paper.) Make a lighter line by not pressing as hard.

- Change your perspective. Hold a sketch upside down or look at it in a mirror. This will help you see things from a different angle so you can know what needs to change.

- A simple, black-and-white sketch can be very striking. You can add color if desired with colored pencils. Berol or Prismacolor are two recommended art brands.

- You can also add color with markers. Pentel is a good brand for art projects.

Using Oil Pastels

- A good, quality oil pastel for beginners is Studio Basic.

- Oil pastels are an excellent, mess-free way to teach the blending of color. Experiment with different colors mixed together.

- Oil pastels work well when layered. Layer colors on top of each other and then scrape away parts of the top layers for an interesting effect.

- Turpentine on a paintbrush can be used to soften the oil pastels and blend them together on the page.

- For broad strokes, lay the pastel on its side and use its length to sweep color across the page.

Using Chalk Pastels

- Studio Basic is good chalk pastel for beginners.

- Chalk pastels can be very dusty. It is probably a good idea to wear old clothes.

- Using actual pastel paper will greatly improve your experience and results with pastels. Colored construction paper also holds chalk better than plain paper.

- Blend and spread color with the tip of your finger, or use a Q-Tip.

- You can erase mistakes, or at least lighten them, with a kneadable eraser.

- Always spray a finished pastel piece with fixative spray. (Hair spray is a cheaper alternative, but be aware that it may yellow the art over time.)

- Use plenty of chalk. No bits of paper should be visible through the chalk.
- For broad strokes, lay the pastel on its side and use its length to sweep color across the page.
- A completed chalk picture can be detailed with white and black charcoal pencils.
- For practice, do a sunset scene. This is an excellent way to learn to blend colors.

Painting

- In the past, younger students were only given large brushes. Research now indicates that they can do better if given a variety of brushes to choose from. It might be best to buy a large reasonably priced bag of mixed brushes for your students. An older student might wish to have a few higher quality brushes.
- Canvases for student painting can be purchased relatively inexpensively. However, it is always a good idea to have a student do a few practice runs on paper before using a canvas. While none of the projects in this book call for canvas, any painting project could be easily adapted to using a canvas.

Painting with Watercolor

- Prang is good beginner's watercolor. Older, more experienced students can use tube watercolor.
- Sometimes tackling a blank page with paints can be very intimidating. To solve this, lightly sketch the desired scene onto the paper using watercolor pencils. The pencils will blend in with the paint.
- Use light colors when starting out. You can always darken it later.
- Use a white crayon on parts of the painting you want to stay white. The crayon will resist the watercolor.
- Use a toothbrush or paintbrush to create a splatter effect on the painting. Simply use your finger to flick the bristles towards the paper. (Cover the part of the painting you don't want splattered with a scrap piece of paper.)

Painting with Tempera

- Premixed versions are often sold as "poster paints." (This is how we refer to the paint in the book.)
- At art supply stores you can also buy dry tempera paint to mix yourself. (Baby food jars work great for storing the mixed paints.) This is only suitable for older students.
- Cake tempera is not recommended.

Using Modeling Clay

Modeling clay is a great hands-on medium for many projects. Here are some tips when using clay:

- Clay can sometimes stick to tabletops. Use a sheet of scrap paper to work with clay. (Wax paper works especially well.)
- Before making a sculpture, it sometimes helps to sketch the design on a piece of paper. Be sure to draw the front, back, and sides.
- Before starting the project, gather some household items to use as aids in shaping the clay. Some suggestions include toothpicks, popsicle sticks, old credit cards, empty film canisters, rolling pins, etc. Use your imagination.

- When making a particularly large sculpture, it might help to make a smaller version first. For example, the Eiffel Tower was built in several smaller versions before the actual construction ever began.
- A large sculpture may also benefit by being built on a form. This saves on clay and makes the object easier to shape. Use wire, popsicle sticks, or aluminum foil to help form the basic shapes of the sculpture.
- Clay needs to be "warmed up" before the actual modeling begins. Knead the clay as you would dough. Push, pull, and squish until the clay is warm and smooth. This will make the modeling process much easier.
- Each type of clay cures or hardens differently. Be sure to follow the directions on the package or recipe for the type of clay you are using. Some modeling clays are designed to stay moist and pliable. These clays are perfect for practice and first attempts at projects.

Types of Clay

There is a wide variety of clay available for purchase. Here is some information on the different types:

Oil-based modeling clay (such as Rose Art): great introductory clay; inexpensive; not very messy; usually does not dry out so it can be reworked.

Sculpey: good clay for detail work; bakes into a plastic-like finish; more expensive than other clays.

Celluclay: actually an instant Paper Mache; can be messy; air dries rather than having to be baked.

PlayFoam: remoldable sculpting beads; available in an assortment of colors; not at all messy; does not dry out; especially good for younger students (obtain from Geography Matters 800-426-4650).

Homemade clay: You can make your own clay at home. Recipes for these six types of clay can be found in the Appendix: basic land clay, sawdust clay, coffee clay, dough clay, edible clay, and play dough.

SAFETY TIPS

Art is meant to be fun and stress free! Follow these tips to keep it that way:
- Keep sharp objects, such as scissors, out of the reach of small children. If your child is old enough to use scissors, always supervise carefully.
- Keep hot irons out of the reach of small children. Only adults or older students under close supervision should use an iron for the art projects in this book.
- Be sure that all paints and other supplies used by little ones are non-toxic. If any toxic paints or supplies are in the house, be sure to keep them put away securely.
- Keep a set of play clothes and an art smock or apron handy for painting and chalk projects. While a majority of art products on the market today are washable, it is better to be safe than sorry.
- Any aerosol sprays, such as fixatives or spray paints, should only be used by adults in well-ventilated areas. Never leave an aerosol can in the reach of a child.
- An adult should always supervise the use of an oven for curing clays.
- Keep a separate set of tools for working with clay and for actual food recipes. For example, it would be unwise to use the same rolling pin to flatten a piece of clay and then flatten dough for biscuits.

TEACHING TIPS

There are several ways you can inspire your child's artistic creativity while they are learning more about foreign cultures. Here are a few ideas:

Taste the culture. Few things get kids more excited than food! Be sure to taste the cuisine of the countries you are studying. Visit a local ethnic restaurant or prepare recipes from the book *Eat Your Way Around the World* by Jamie Aramini. The FoodLink icon next to country names is a reminder.

Hear the music. While your kids are busy creating their art projects, play a little ethnic music to help inspire them. Visit your local library to see their selection of world music. If they don't have what you are looking for, ask the librarian to request it though the Interlibrary Loan program. You can also visit worldmusic.nationalgeographic.com and www.smithsonianglobalsound.org for a wide selection of music from around the world.

Dress the part. A great way to inspire your student artists is to put them in native dress. Their art will feel more authentic because they look the part. It doesn't have to be an elaborate ensemble. It could be as simple as a sheet wrapped like a Greek toga or a sombrero for Latin America.

See the art. Many museums and art galleries have entire sections devoted to world art. Check to see what displays are available in your area. You might also be able to see native art in the home of someone who has visited a foreign country. Check with local churches to see if any missionaries might be willing to share their experiences and cultural art with you.

TIPS FOR TEACHING GROUPS

Geography Through Art is an excellent resource to teach world art in a group setting. Here are some helpful hints for your classroom, homeschool co-op, or other group.

World art tour. Go through the book project by project for a complete world art tour or have each student select a different project from the book to do at home and bring to class.

World art exhibition. When your students have completed their study of world art, host an exhibition of their works. Have them invite friends, family, and loved ones. Other student groups may also wish to come because it is sure to be an educational experience. Have students prepare poster boards with information about each country and culture. Display these alongside their artworks. Be sure to serve a selection of international foods as well. Students may wish to dress in ethnic clothing that matches the country where their art originated.

World art class. If you have worked through the entire book, or most of it, your students should be well versed in art and culture around the world. Let them share their knowledge with a group of younger students. Have your students prepare lessons to share along with the projects.

Local artists. You may be able to invite local artists to speak to your group. Let them share with you their knowledge of international arts, as well as practical skills to improve the artwork of the students.

Video documentaries. Check with your local library for video documentaries about world cultures. View these before starting a new project to help students gain a better understanding of life around the world.

SUPPLIES

Each project begins with a materials list. Here is a basic list of supplies that are used most often. You may want to obtain any that you do not already have.

Basic Art Materials

acrylic paints	glue	scissors
brown craft paper	hole punch	stapler
cardstock	markers	string
cardboard or foam board	paintbrushes, many sizes	tape
chalk	empty paper towel rolls or	tempura paints
clay	wrapping paper rolls	toothpicks
colored pencils	pencils	tracing paper
construction paper	poster board	watercolor paints
crayons	poster paints	watercolor paper
drawing paper	ruler	yarn or ribbon

All of the art supplies needed to complete these projects should be available for purchase at your local discount or hobby store. You can also visit the following websites to purchase art supplies:

www.dickblick.com A huge selection of art supplies available at affordable prices.

www.crizmac.com   An excellent resource for world art projects, their catalog includes books, prints, and actual folk art samples from countries all over the world. They also sell compact discs of world music and videos showing world art and the artists who create it.

Recommended Geography Resources
Intermediate World Atlas or a student world atlas
Almanac
Geography Terms Chart
Eat Your Way Around the World by Jamie Aramini

WORLD

World Summary

The study of geography covers a broad range of topics and includes lands, climate, terrain, people, culture, places, mapping, flora, fauna, and more. It can be divided into the study of the planet earth (physical geography) and the study of people and cultures (human geography). In *Geography Through Art* you will glimpse the human geography of the world by learning about cultures and people groups through their art.

Use the map in each continent section to locate where your art projects originate. There is an outline map of each continent in the Appendix for you to label. Feel free to add other places of interest beyond where your art lessons take you.

Over 190 nations call Earth their home. The earth is the third planet from the sun in our galaxy. It has the perfect mix of water, oxygen, light, heat, and minerals to support life. The earth's surface is 71% water and 29% land. The five largest bodies of water are Pacific Ocean, Atlantic Ocean, Indian Ocean, Southern Ocean, and Arctic Ocean. The largest portions of land, called continents, are Asia, Africa, North America, South America, Antarctica, Europe, and Australia. The Pacific Islands together with Australia are often referred to as the continent of Oceania.

Facts

Area total: 197 million square miles

Area land: 57.5 million square miles (16 times the size of the United States)

Area water: 139.4 million square miles

Highest point: Mount Everest, 29.028 ft.

Lowest point: Dead Sea, -1374 ft. (Antarctica's Bentley Subglacial Trench is -8327 ft. but is under ice and considered subterranean.)

Lowest ocean depth: Mariana Trench, 6.8 miles below the surface of the Pacific Ocean

Longest river: Nile, 4132 miles

River carrying the largest volume of water: Amazon discharges 7.7 cu ft./second

Largest country by area: Russia

Largest country by population: China

Languages (first language only): 13.2% Mandarin Chinese; 4.9% Spanish; 4.7% English; 3.1% Arabic; 2.7% Hindi; 2.7% Portuguese; 2.6% Bengali; 2.2% Russian; 1.9% Japanese

Religions: 33% Christian; 21% Muslim; 13% Hindu; 6% Buddhist

World

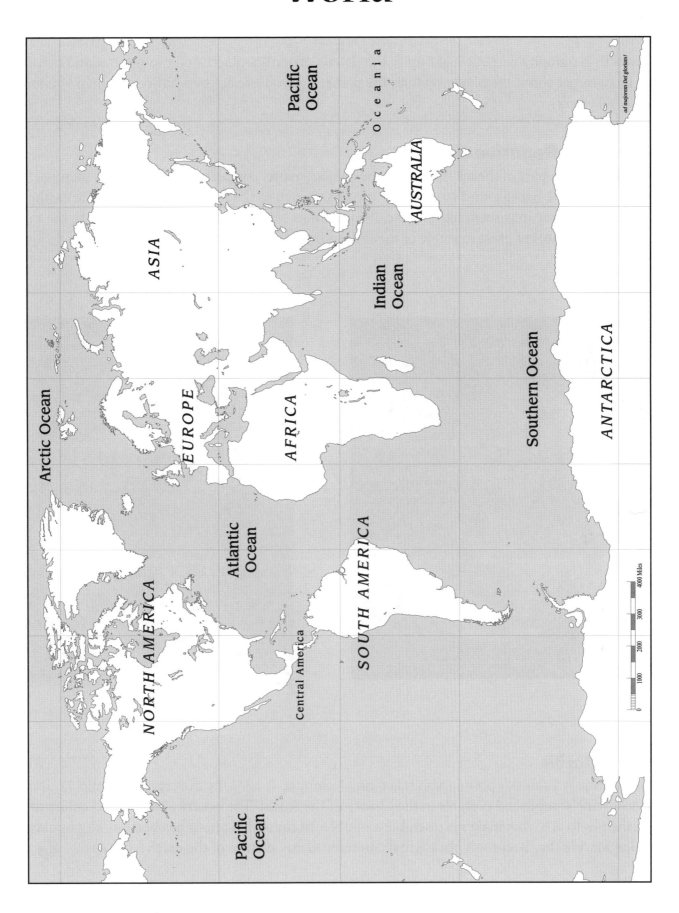

GEOGRAPHY THROUGH ART

THE PLANET EARTH

Sometimes in geography we get caught up in the details of continents, rivers, mountains, and oceans, causing us to forget about the bigger picture: the planet Earth. Here are two projects to help you look at the earth as a whole.

Positive and Negative Space

Positive space is the part of the art filled with the subject matter, such as the earth in this picture. **Negative space** is the background space in a piece of art, such as the black space beyond the earth. While a negative space may seem like a waste, it sometimes serves to draw more attention to the main part of the work. Another great example of this is Rembrandt's Self-Portrait.

The Blue Marble

The Blue Marble is a famous photograph taken on December 7, 1972, by the crew of Apollo 17. It is one of the most widely published pictures in the history of the world. The beauty and blended colors of the earth in the photo are what makes it resemble a marble. Because this photo has become so popular, the term "Blue Marble" has become a phrase that can refer to any picture of the earth from space.

Earth from Space ☆

This is a great lesson in positive and negative space. The planet represents positive space and the background is negative space.

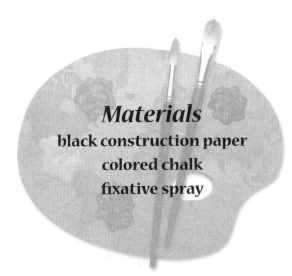

Materials
black construction paper
colored chalk
fixative spray

1. Using chalk, color a picture of the earth on the black paper. Looking at the photo of the earth, try to mimic the natural shading, shadow, and texture. This will help the earth look more three dimensional.

2. When you have completed your picture, seal your work using fixative spray. Let dry.

Note: Fixative spray is available in the arts and crafts section of your local hobby or department store. It is used as a sealant for several different kinds of art work. Hair spray is often used as an alternative. If you choose to use hair spray, be aware that it could yellow your art over time.

The Third Dimension

Drawing the planet earth on paper is an example of **one dimensional** art. This means that the art is flat. You can try to make a one dimensional piece look like it is **three dimensional** through different effects such as shading. Real three dimensional art, however, has height, width, and depth. It is by no means flat! Sculptures or the paper mache globe project below are three dimensional. Look around your house, and make a list of one and three dimensional items.

Paper Mache Globe ☆☆

Paper mache was originally a French term meaning "chewed up paper." It can be done with a variety of pastes and materials. If you enjoy this project, search online for more paper mache projects, or visit your local library for a book on the topic.

Materials
1 cup flour
1 cup water
1 tablespoon salt
newspaper strips
1 round balloon, inflated
tempera paints
spray varnish

1. Stir together flour, salt, and water until mixture forms a thick glue-like paste.

2. Dip and thoroughly cover newspaper strips with flour mixture. Place on balloon, each strip overlapping the edge of the last.

3. When the balloon is completely covered, let it dry for twenty-four hours. Repeat this process two more times for a sturdy globe.

4. When your globe has thoroughly dried, paint on the continents and decorate as desired. To seal your project, use a spray varnish.

You have just made a three-dimensional representation of the planet earth! Hold your paper mache globe next to your earth drawing and notice the difference.

ALL ABOUT MAPS

Cartography is the art and science of making maps. Map making is a large part of geography. We use maps often for directions. You will use a map at the amusement park, for example, to find your way to all the shows and rides. Maps play an important role in our day-to-day life. What you may not realize is that maps can also be a form of art. On this page is a very old world map. As you can see, all of the intricate detail makes it into a beautiful work of art. Here are a few fun projects you can do with maps.

Pangea Puzzle ☆☆

Scientists believe that when the continents were first formed, they were all together in one big continent, called "Pangea." It wasn't until later that the continents separated to form the continents we know today. To make your own Pangea puzzle, follow the instructions below.

Materials
world map
tracing paper
pencil
scissors
cardstock
glue
colored pencils or markers

1. Using your pencil and tracing paper, trace the continents from the world map.

2. Glue your continents onto cardstock and then cut them out. (This makes them easier to handle.)

3. Label and decorate the continents as desired.

4. Once step three is completed, try to piece the continents together just like a puzzle. Notice, for example, how South America seems to fit into the contour of the African continent. Store your continents in a folder or sandwich bag so you can let other people try putting together the puzzle, too. You might also find them handy for tracing if you ever need to draw a continent for a school project.

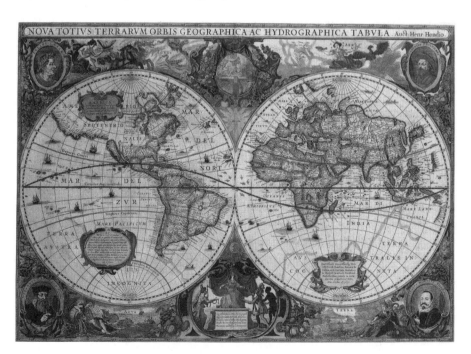

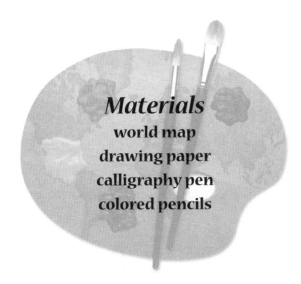

Materials
world map
drawing paper
calligraphy pen
colored pencils

Make a World Map ☆☆

1. Trace a world map, or use your Pangea puzzle continents. If you prefer, you can make a copy of the world outline map in the Appendix.

2. Label the continents using your calligraphy pen.

3. Color the continents using your colored pencils. Don't be limited to blue for water and green for land. Use your imagination. Make your map into a masterpiece! You can even add a decorative border if you would like.

Make a Treasure Map ☆☆

Making a map of your own is a great way to understand how difficult map making can be. Cartographers of the past didn't have outline maps that simply needed the blanks filled in. They had to start from scratch, much like you will in this treasure map activity.

Materials
a small "treasure"
(such as a toy, candy, or money)
brown colored pencil
watercolor paper
watercolor paints
paintbrushes

1. Pick a spot to hold your treasure hunt. This could be somewhere in your house, yard, or (with your parent's permission) neighborhood. Hide the treasure.

2. Using the brown pencil, draw a map of the area surrounding the buried treasure. Use symbols to label important spots on the map, such as trees, roads, furniture, rooms, or buildings. Remember to put an "X" where your treasure is hidden!

3. Use watercolors to paint what you have drawn. Try to paint every space on the map until no more of the blank paper can be seen.

4. Let someone (such as a friend, sibling, or parent) use the map to find the hidden treasure. Afterwards, you may want to frame the map to put on your bedroom wall.

Artist Profile: MERCATOR

Gerardus Mercator was a Flemish mapmaker born in 1512. He is most famous for developing a style of mapmaking that greatly aided sailors in navigating the globe. Because of Mercator's maps, travel at sea became much safer. Although his maps made world travel easier, they also distorted the actual size of the continents. Europe, for example, looks much larger on a Mercator map than it really is in comparison to other continents. Because of this, his style of mapmaking is seldom used around the world today. ⓘ

How to Age Your Maps

If you want to make your maps look older than they really are, here are a couple of things to do. Try to think of other things you could do to age your maps.

1. Tear off the smooth edges of your map. If the torn edges aren't perfectly even, it will look better.

2. Fold the map into a small square that would fit in your pocket. Make the creases extra sharp. This will help your map look as if it has been carried around in someone's pocket for a long time!

3. Unfold the map and paint on a thin coat of tea. You can use a paintbrush or just the tea bag if you want.

4. Crumple up the map and let dry overnight.

5. Unfold the map and brush with a thin coat of vegetable oil. Let dry. You now have a map that looks like it has been around a really long time.

Map Resources

The U.S. Geological Survey has several excellent resources on the history of maps and more. Contact them at this address (or visit them on the web at www.usgs.gov/):

Geological Survey
Information Services
P.O. Box 25286
Denver, CO 80225

Ask for:

• Map Adventures Teacher's Packet

• Map Projections

• Planetary Maps

• USGS Maps.

COUNTRY PROJECTS

Most projects in this book represent the art and culture of specific countries. However, there are some projects that are suitable to do for any country.

- Complete the Countries of the World Fact Sheet in the Appendix for any country you study.
- Cook a meal associated with countries you study using *Eat Your Way Around the World* by Jamie Aramini. Watch for the FoodLink icon  as a reminder that a meal for that country is included in this cookbook.
- Make a travel poster.
- Draw the flag.

Travel Posters

A travel poster is a great project to make when you are studying a country. It should be eye-catching and easy to read. It should highlight one (or a few) of the main attractions a country has to offer. A travel poster is a great conclusion to the study of a country. It will help you show what you have learned about the country.

Materials
poster board
pencil
ruler
markers
poster paints

1. Decide on a country and a design for your poster. You may want to sketch the design on a scrap piece of paper first. Consider doing a landscape or cityscape.

2. Draw your design on the poster board in pencil. Use a ruler to make large, easy-to-read letters.

3. Use markers and/or poster paints to add color. Remember to use bright colors that will easily grab attention.

World Flags

The flag of each country is unique and makes for a fun art project. Research the flags in an almanac, encyclopedia, or on the Internet.

Materials
paper
pencil
ruler
markers

1. On a sheet of paper, trace or draw in pencil the flag design for the country you are studying. Use a ruler to ensure that your lines are straight.

2. Color the flag with markers. (You may wish to look up what the flag colors symbolize.)

3. When you are finished, put the flag in your geography notebook.

AFRICA

Continent Summary

Africa is the 2nd largest continent in the world. It is generally divided into two regions: North Africa and south of the Sahara. It has many climate changes and contrasts. The hottest temperature recorded in the world was 136° in 1992 in Libya. Have you ever been in temperatures over 100°?

Africa is known for its diversity of animals and plants. The Serengeti, in northern Tanzania, is a vast plain of grassland, acacia bushes, forests, and rocky outcrops. The Serengeti National Park has been set aside as a protected area for African wildlife. If you were to visit the park, you'd see antelope, buffalo, cheetahs, elephants, gazelles, giraffes, hyenas, leopards, lions, black rhinoceros, and zebras. Chimpanzees, gorillas, and many birds make their homes in the forests of Central and Western Africa.

The world's largest desert takes up a vast amount of northern Africa where the climate is arid. It is the Sahara Desert, which covers nearly the same amount of space as the United States. The camel is still the preferred mode of transportation in the Sahara as it is well suited for the climate and desert conditions.

Some other geographical features of interest include the Great Rift Valley in the east which is surrounded by a number of plateaus; volcanic eruptions and elongated lakes and valleys along the rift; the Atlas Mountains in the northwest. The highest elevation in Africa is at Kilimanjaro where the mountain peak rises over 19,000 feet above sea level.

Africa is surrounded by the Atlantic Ocean on the west, Indian Ocean on the east, and the Mediterranean Sea on the north. Africa boasts the longest river in the world, the Nile, which flows north through Uganda, South Sudan, Sudan, and Egypt. The banks of the Nile flood yearly, leaving rich deposits of fresh fertile silt. This annual soil replenishment provided for abundant agriculture for thousands of years. Other major rivers are the Congo, in the midst of the Democratic Republic of the Congo (formerly Zaire), and the Zambezi, running through western Zambia. Africa's largest lake, the beautiful Lake Victoria, is not too far from Serengeti National Park.

A discovery along the banks of the Orange River near Hopetown in 1867 marked a turning point in South Africa's history. Can you guess what it was? A 21-carat diamond! This area eventually became the diamond capital of the world. South Africa boasts the world's greatest deposits of gold, chromite, manganese, and platinum metals.

Facts
Size: 11,700,000 square miles
Rank: 2nd largest continent
Highest point: Kilimanjaro 19,319 ft.
Lowest point: Lake Assal, Djibouti, 512 ft. below sea level
Main rivers: Nile, Congo, Zambezi
Largest country: Algeria
Smallest country: Seychelles
Main languages: Arabic, English, French, Portuguese

Africa

ATLANTIC OCEAN

Str. of Gibraltar

Canary Is.

MOROCCO

TUNISIA

ATLAS MOUNTAINS

MEDITERRANEAN SEA

Alexandria

ALGERIA

LIBYA

Western
Desert

EGYPT

Nile

RED SEA

Tropic of Cancer

WESTERN
SAHARA

Mt. Tahat ▲

SAHARA   DESERT

Libyan Desert

Nubian
Desert

MAURITANIA

MALI

NIGER

CHAD

SUDAN

ERITREA

Lake
Assal

DJIBOUTI

Gulf of Aden

Sénégal

SENEGAL

Niger

BURKINO FASO

JEBEL
MARRA

Blue Nile

ETHIOPIAN HIGHLANDS

SOMALIA

GAMBIA

GUINEA-BISSAU

GUINEA

SIERRA
LEONE

LIBERIA

IVORY
COAST

GHANA

TOGO

BENIN

NIGERIA

CAMEROON

SOUTH
SUDAN

White Nile

ETHIOPIA

Accra

GULF OF GUINEA

EQUATORIAL GUINEA

CENTRAL
AFRICAN
REPUBLIC

Congo

Margherita Peak ▲

UGANDA

KENYA

▲ Kirinyaga

CONGO

GABON

DEMOCRATIC REPUBLIC
OF THE CONGO

RWANDA

BURUNDI

Lake
Victoria

Kilimanjaro ▲

INDIAN OCEAN

ATLANTIC OCEAN

ANGOLA
PLATEAU

ANGOLA

ZAMBIA

Zambezi

TANZANIA

MALAWI

MOZAMBIQUE

Mozambique Channel

NAMIBIA

Okavango
Delta

ZIMBABWE

MADAGASCAR

Namib Desert

BOTSWANA

Kalahari
Desert

SWAZILAND

Tropic of Capricorn

Orange

LESOTHO

SOUTH AFRICA

ad majorem Dei gloriam!

0   500   1000 Miles

GEOGRAPHY THROUGH ART

AFRICA

Masks ☆☆ ⓘ

Masks are an important part of African tribal culture. Richly decorated masks have been an important part of tribal and religious ceremonies for many years. The masks are usually carved from wood, painted, and accented with gemstones, ivory, or other items.

1. Lay a piece of cardstock on the table. Place your head, facedown, on the cardstock. Have someone trace the general shape of your face. This ensures that your mask is the proper fit.

2. Cut your mask out, following the traced lines. Decorate your mask. Look online or in a book at samples of African masks to help you get the idea.

Materials
cardstock
pencil
scissors
natural colored twine or raffia
tape
poster or acrylic paints
paintbrushes
hole punch

3. Tape strands of raffia or twine to the back side of your mask if you want your mask to have hair. Cut out holes for your eyes if you plan on wearing the mask.

4. Use your hole punch to put holes on both sides of the mask. Tie a long strand of twine or raffia to each hole. Have someone tie the mask to your face, or simply tie the strands together to hang on the wall.

☆ Primary students can skip the cutting step. Instead, use a paper or Styrofoam plate for the mask.

☆☆☆ Secondary students might try making their mask from paper mache.

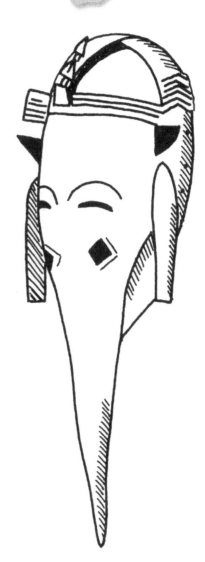

Sculpture

The people of Africa have a great heritage in primitive sculpture. Look at the samples on this page. Each region of the continent has different types and techniques of sculpture that are popular. The sculptures are usually woodcarvings, but we will make ours out of modeling clay.

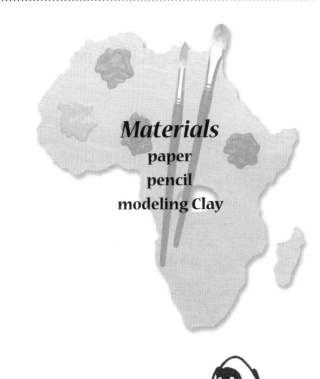

Materials
paper
pencil
modeling Clay

1. Sketch a design on paper of what you want your sculpture to look like. Try to make a design that looks like some of the African ones below. Look online or in a book about Africa for more inspiration.

2. Sculpt your design using modeling clay. Use a wood-toned color such as brown or tan. You can use toothpicks or disposable plastic silverware to help sculpt smaller details.

3. Dry or bake your clay according to the directions that came with the clay.

Ghana

Congo

Ivory Coast

Nigeria

CENTRAL AFRICAN REPUBLIC

Collage

A **collage** is a picture put together of many different parts. For example, the sun in a collage would be made of many different kinds of yellow paper. The grass would be created from many different kinds of green paper. To make a collage, you can use patterned scrapbooking papers. You can also use the pages of an outdated magazine or calendar, with your parent's permission.

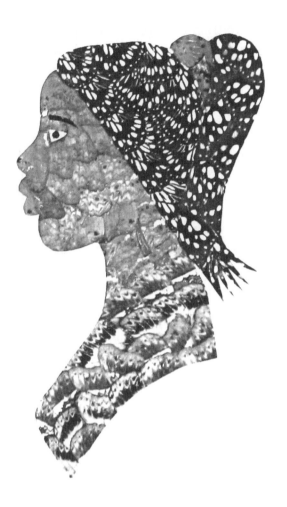

Materials
patterned papers in a variety of colors
pencils
scissors
glue
cardstock

Butterfly Wing Art ☆☆

Butterfly wing art is a common folk art in the Central African Republic. Each picture is composed of many delicate butterfly wings. (The wings come from butterflies that are not endangered and that have lived out their natural life span.) The wings are carefully arranged to create a beautiful scene or animal.

1. Decide what picture you want to make for your collage. You might choose an African animal such as a zebra, lion, or giraffe. You could also make a picture of an African tree or flower. Look on the Internet or in a library book for images of Africa to give you some ideas.

2. Lightly sketch your picture onto a piece of cardstock. Big, bold shapes will be easier to collage than small details. Write inside each shape what color you want it to be.

3. Select papers in the colors you will need for your collage. Cut or tear your papers into small pieces.

4. Glue the colored papers onto your cardstock. Use the colors you wrote in earlier as a guide.

5. You can color in the background if you want. Butterfly Wing Art usually has a plain white background so that the wings stand out boldly from the page.

QUICKSKETCH: ZEBRA

What is the first animal that comes to your mind when you think of Africa? Is it the zebra? The zebra, a member of the horse family, is a beautiful animal covered with black and white stripes. The stripes are not only beautiful, but serve a purpose as well. The stripes help the zebra blend in when standing in a grove of trees. Some scientists believe the stripes also make the zebra look like blades of grass in a field to the color-blind lion. In your geography notebook, draw a picture of a zebra. Pay close attention to how you place your stripes. A zebra's stripes are vertical everywhere except on its back end and legs, where the stripes are horzontal. To make your zebra stand out even more in your picture, put it in front of a beautiful African sunset of reds, oranges, and yellows.

EGYPT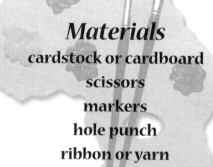

Hieroglyphics ☆

The written language of the ancient Egyptians is referred to as **hieroglyphics**. It is made up of symbols that represented a word. Over time, certain symbols came to represent certain sounds, much like our own letters do today. The names of royalty, such as the pharaoh, were always written inside an oval. This oval was called a **cartouche**. For this project, create a cartouche using your own name.

Materials
cardstock or cardboard
scissors
markers
hole punch
ribbon or yarn

1. Cut an oval shape out of cardboard or cardstock. Egyptians often wrote vertically, so you can write from top to bottom if desired.

2. Design your own hieroglyphs. What symbols do people think of when they hear your name? Is it a soccer ball? A ballerina slipper? A smile? A frown? Choose a few of the things that best represent you and use those as your symbols. Write your name inside the oval using hieroglyphics.

3. Decorate your cartouche with markers.

4. Punch a hole in the top of the cartouche and tie a piece of ribbon or yarn through the hole. You are now ready to hang the cartouche on your bedroom door or in your room.

Profile

A profile is a portrait of a person done using the side view. Instead of looking someone squarely in the face, you are looking at the person from the side. Profiles were very popular in ancient Egyptian art.

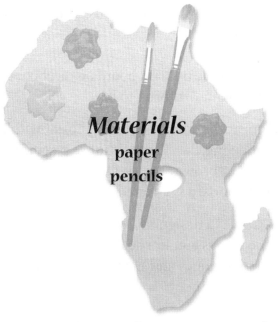

Materials
paper
pencils

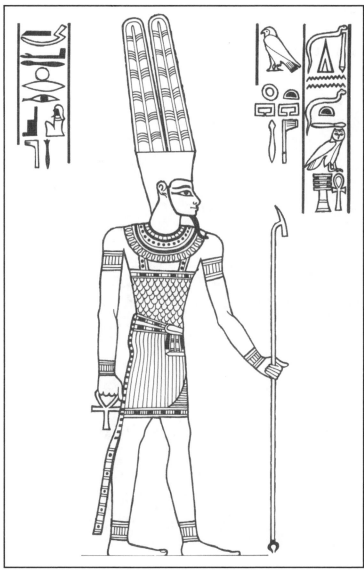

Egyptian-Style Drawing ☆

Egyptian art is unique. It has a simple, outline style that is rarely found in the art of other cultures. Using the example on this page, draw an Egyptian portrait.

1. Look at the picture on this page. Study the details to help you get some ideas for your own picture.

2. Draw the outline of a body from the side. Be sure the feet are also sideways.

3. Fill in the details of an Egyptian face. Notice the dark makeup lines around the eyes.

4. Add details like clothes and jewelry. You might also want to add some hieroglyphics to make your picture feel more authentic.

Carved Orthostat ☆☆

An **orthostat** is a large rock that has been placed in a vertical position. The ancient Egyptians frequently carved orthostats with pictures and hieroglyphics. We have learned a lot about ancient Egyptian culture by looking at the orthostat depictions. You can make your own version at home.

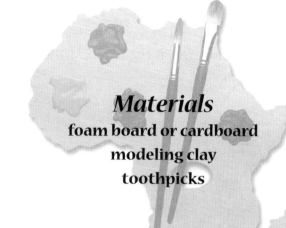

Materials
foam board or cardboard
modeling clay
toothpicks

1. Cut a piece of foam board or cardboard to the size you want your orthostat to be.

2. Smear the surface of the orthostat with a thin layer of modeling clay. (Try to choose a neutral, rock-like color such as brown, tan, or grey.) Be sure the entire surface of the board is covered.

3. "Carve" a design into your clay using toothpicks. Use the things you learned in the first two lessons about hieroglyphics and Egyptian drawings to add interest to your carving.

QUICKSKETCH: CAT

The Egyptian word for cat was myeo or mau. Ancient Egyptians were the first known people to keep cats as pets. In fact, the cat was actually considered a god in Egypt. The Egyptian love for cats is seen frequently in their art. The people made carvings and paintings of cats, as well as crafting jewelry and furniture in the shape of a cat. The Egyptians treasured cats so much that killing a cat was punishable by death. When a cat did die of natural causes, it was mummified just like a person would have been. Egyptian soldiers were even told to take cats from other countries and bring them back to their "true" home, Egypt. Draw a picture of a cat in your geography notebook.

QUICKSKETCH: PYRAMIDS OF GIZA

Some of the most interesting sights in Egypt are the Great Pyramids at Giza. Pyramids are probably one of the first things you think of when you think of Egypt. The Pyramids are the only surviving wonder from the Seven Wonders of the Ancient World. Draw a picture in your student notebook of the Great Pyramids.

GHANA

The Legend of the Kente Cloth

The Kente cloth has existed for many years in Ghana and the surrounding regions of Africa, but how did it originate? How did the idea to weave this beautiful cloth get started? An African legend says that two brothers were walking when they came upon a spider web. They watched in awe as the spider wove a piece of the beautiful web. When they returned home, they decided to weave something of their own. The resulting kente cloth was so beautiful that the king of the country had to have it for himself. The brothers were then hired by the king to make the cloths just for him and his family.

Kente Cloth Color Symbols

White: purity   Black: maturity   Green: growth
Yellow: wealth   Blue: peace   Red: struggle

Kente Cloth ☆☆

The kente cloth is an African ceremonial cloth. It was originally worn only by members of the ruling family. It is woven on a special loom by people in the country of Ghana. Each color used in a kente cloth has a special symbolic meaning. This project will help you "weave" your own paper version of the kente cloth.

Materials
construction paper in varying colors
scissors
glue

1. Select a main color for a kente cloth from your construction paper. Cut slits into the paper as shown in the example.

2. Choose the other colors you will use for your kente cloth. Look at the list above to see what different colors represent. Cut strips from the construction paper colors you have chosen. The strips should be about one inch wide and run the length of the paper.

3. Weave one of the paper strips through the top of the slits. It should go under the first row, over the next, under, over, etc. Glue the ends of the strip to the paper.

4. Weave another paper strip in a different color. This time weave it over the first row, under the next, over, under, etc. Glue the ends to the paper.

5. Repeat steps three and four until you have filled up the paper.

Cut on lines

Golden Staff Finials ★★★

For hundreds of years, the people of Ghana were known for their works of art using gold. They created gold jewelry, sculptures, and staff finials. (A staff finial is the decorative top to a walking stick.) This art was created as a result of the overwhelming abundance of gold in the country of Ghana. These finials were created using the "lost wax" method of casting. Finials were often in the form of animals, people, or plants.

Materials
dowel rod or walking stick
air dry modeling clay
gold paint
paintbrush

1. At the top of the dowel rod or walking stick, make a decorative finial out of modeling clay. (Use a light-colored clay such as white or tan.) Let dry thoroughly.

2. Paint the finial with gold paint. Let dry.

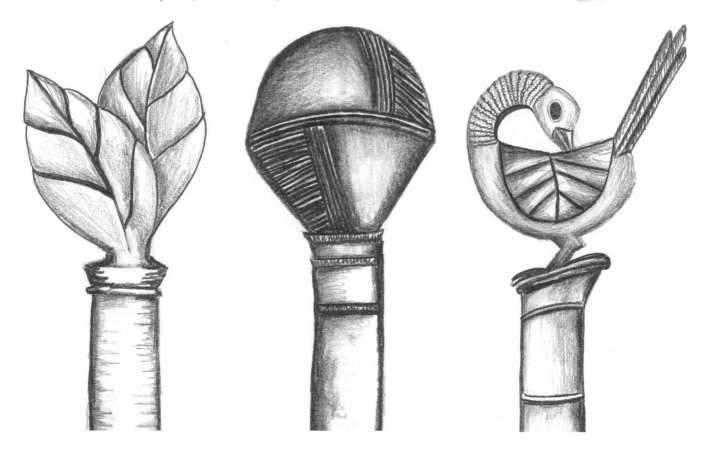

Lost Wax Casting

Lost wax casting is a process of casting wax into molds for making metal items such as finials, sculptures, or tools. This method of casting was used by Africans for many centuries. The first step in lost wax casting was to carve a design out of wax. The design was then covered with clay and baked over a hot fire. A small hole at the base of the design would allow the wax to melt and flow out the bottom. (Hence the name "lost wax.") After the baked design cooled, it was filled through the hole with gold. Once the gold hardened, the clay was broken to reveal the final piece.

Coffin Art

Ghana is also known for another form of art beside the kente cloth and gold casting. It is something a little more bizarre—custom coffins. In the capital city of Accra, a handful of artists make coffins specially customized for a client's occupation or interest. A lobster fisherman might choose a lobster coffin. A chief would probably choose an eagle. A cattle herdsmen might want his coffin to be that of a bull. These items not only celebrate the lives of the departed, but also reflect their social status. According to the September 1994 issue of National Geographic, one of these coffins costs on average $400.00. That is an entire year's salary in Ghana! ⓘ

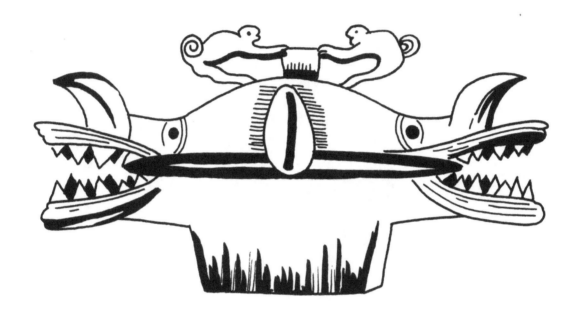

TANZANIA

Mount Kilimanjaro, Tanzania ★☆

Mount Kilimanjaro is the tallest, and perhaps most famous, mountain in Africa. Its name translates into "large rock." Look at the picture of the mountain on this page. Are you surprised to see the snow at the top? Even though Africa has a very warm climate, Mt. Kilimanjaro is still topped with snow because of the high elevation. You can draw a picture of the mountain in your geography notebook, or try this project to make a three-dimensional version.

Materials
heavy cardboard or foam board
2 cups salt
2 cups flour
1 1/3 cups water
poster or acrylic paint
glue
pebbles or stones
sand
cotton balls

1. Study the picture of Mt. Kilimanjaro. Look online or in a book for more pictures if you want to study the mountain further.

2. Cut your cardboard or foam board a little larger than the base of your mountain.

3. Mix together the salt, flour, and water thoroughly to form salt dough. Use the mixture to form a three-dimensional version of Mt. Kilimanjaro on the board. Try to stay as close as possible to the pictures you have seen.

4. When the salt dough mountain has dried, paint it to match the picture. You can also embellish it by adding cotton balls for snow, pebbles for rocks, and sand around the base. Use your imagination.

Mount Kilimanjaro, Kenya

Topography

Topography is the study of the way land lays. It is the shape of the surface of a land area. In landscape art, topography is very important. It helps make your picture look more **realistic** if the topography is correct.

MOROCCO 🍴

Rug Making

Have you ever heard of a flying carpet? North African rugs can't really fly, but they are so beautiful that it is no wonder such a legend exists. There are different techniques used, including knotting the rug or weaving it on a loom. Many women make rugs at home to sell at market or use themselves. On the next page, you can see pictures of what a loom might look like, as well as some sample rugs. Notice the patterns on the rugs. These geometric patterns are full of squares, triangles, lines, diamonds, etc. Make a rug with a similar pattern in this project.

Materials
graph paper
colored pencils

1. Use graph paper to design your own African rug. (You can use your own graph paper or make a copy of the graph paper in the Appendix.)

2. Use colored pencils to make the design. Every square must be colored. Try to imagine what it would be like if you were weaving your design rather than just coloring it.

Figure A: A typical Bedouin loom 1. Beams, 2. Uprights, 3. Cords attaching the upper beam to the uprights, 4. Straining nails, 5. Stretchers, 6. Shed stick, 7. Reeds in the warp

Figure B: Bedouin carpet design with a rectangular field divided into three sections.

Figure C: Bedouin carpet design with a rectangular field divided into four sections separated by strong borders.

Figure D: Bedouin carpet design with a series of compartments running length-wise

Figure A

Figure B

Figure C

Figure D

ZIMBABWE

Animal Art ☆

Artists have a tendency to put their surroundings into their art. It should come as no surprise, then, that animals are a common theme in African art. The beautiful and richly varied creatures of the African continent make an excellent subject for any piece of art, whether it be sculpting, painting, or drawing. These animals were drawn in Zimbabwe and other countries in eastern Africa. They are excellent examples of positive and negative space. (See the lesson on the planet earth for more information on positive and negative space.)

Materials
white construction paper
black construction paper
white chalk
black marker

1. On the white paper, copy one of the animals on this page using a black marker. The zebra would be a good choice. You can see that the black part of the animal is the positive space, the space the artwork uses. The white part is the negative space.

2. On the black paper, copy the same animal using the white chalk. (You should be drawing the exact opposite lines from what you drew last time.) Now the white part of the animal has become the positive space! Which color was easier to do? Which one looks better once completed?

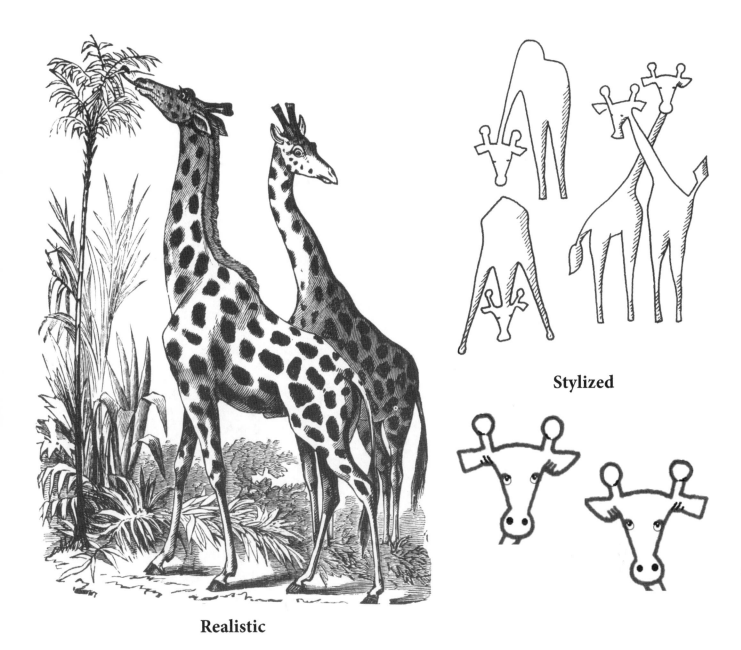

Stylized

Realistic

QuickSketch: Giraffe

One of Africa's most fascinating animals has a large population in Kenya. It is the giraffe. Giraffes are characterized by their long necks and their unique spots, both of which serve a purpose. Giraffes use their long necks to eat leaves from tall trees. Their spots are a form of camouflage that helps protect them from predators. On this page, you see two different giraffe drawings. One is a realistic drawing. It looks similar to a real picture of a giraffe. The other picture is a **stylized** drawing. It is a simple drawing of a giraffe that highlights its main features. This is the kind of giraffe you might see in African folk art. In your geography notebook, draw a picture of a giraffe. You can draw a realistic giraffe, a stylized giraffe, or one of each.

QUICKSKETCH: LION

The lion is another famous African animal. This huge cat is found on the continents of Africa and Asia. It is easily recognizable because of its distinct mane. Scientists say that the mane helps the lion look more powerful to its prey by making it look bigger than it really is. Draw a lion in your geography notebook. You can draw a female lion, without a mane, or a male lion with a mane. Try to draw the lion roaring. How can you show the lion's roar in a picture? Use your imagination. Perhaps draw a person in the picture responding in fear to the roar. You could also draw some leaves of a tree waving in the path of the roar.

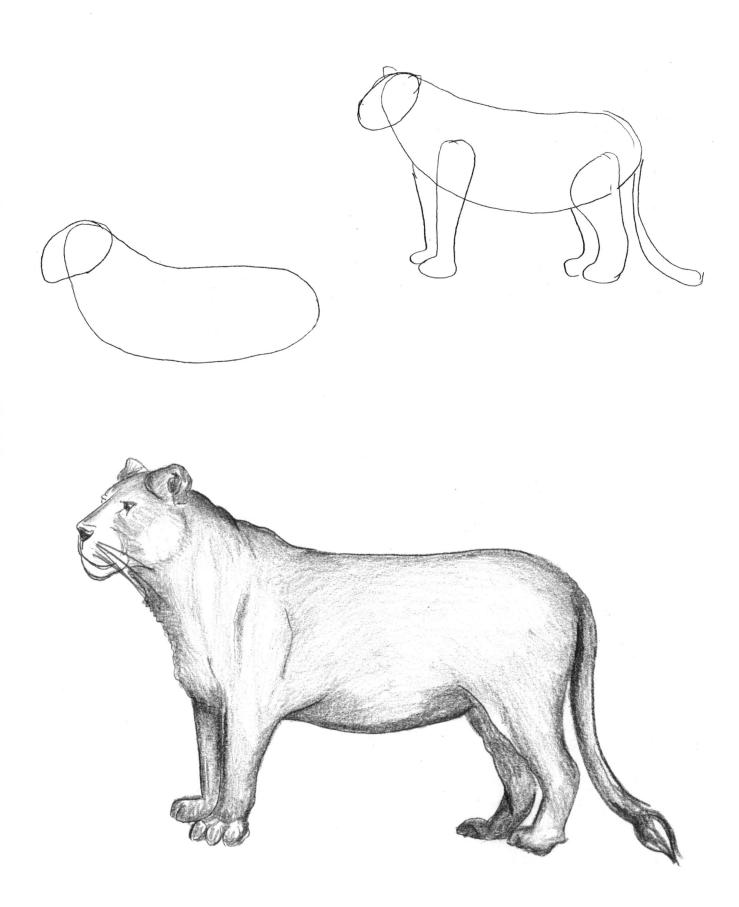

ASIA

Continent Summary

Asia is the largest continent in the world. It is separated from Europe by the Ural and Caucasus Mountians. It has over 78,000 miles of coastline and is comprised of 46 countries. The largest country in the world is in both Asia and Euorpe. It stretches over 11 time zones. Can you guess the name of the country? Russia!

The world's highest peak is in Asia. Mount Everest in the Himalayas rises to a height of over 29,000 feet. The lowest point in Asia is also the lowest point on earth. It is on the shore of the Dead Sea, 1349 feet below sea level. The Dead Sea is not really a sea at all but is a salt lake between the countries of Israel and Jordan.

The world's largest inland body of water is not really a sea but is actually Asia's largest lake, the Capsian Sea. Did you know that the Caspian Sea is situated at about 92 feet below sea level? It was part of an important commercial trade route during the Middle Ages. You may be interested in further study on the Caspian Sea.

Over 40% of the world's oil is produced in Asia. The continent also has more than 20% of the world's gold. Caviar and oil are obtained from Asia's Eastern shore. The main languages spoken in Asia include Arabic, Chinese, English, and Russian.

The land making up Asia is very diverse. It not only boasts the world's highest mountain and the lowest lake but also is home to the Great Plateau of Tibet (China), the Gobi Desert in Mongolia, the deserts of Syria and the Arabian Peninsula, the Deccan Plateau in Southern India, and many volcanic peaks in Kamchatka and Japan. The three great rivers of China are called Huang (Yellow), Yangtze (Chang), and Xi. Two other well-known rivers in Turkey and Iraq are the Euphrates and the Tigris.

Asia is such a big continent it is often divided into smaller regions when studying or mapping.

- **Middle East:** crossroads of three continents (Europe, Africa, and Asia); mostly desert; birthplace of the world's three most influential religions (Christianity, Islam, and Judaism).

- **South Asia:** India, Bangladesh, Pakistan, Nepal, Bhutan, and Sri Lanka; diverse physically and subject to devastating cyclones and monsoon rains; home to the highest mountains in the world.

- **Southeast Asia:** a region of islands and peninsulas in the far southeastern corner of Asia; tropical, hot, and wet with rain forests and mountains.

- **East Asia:** China, Mongolia, and North Korea; home to one fifth of the world's population.

Facts
Size: 17,212,000 square miles
Rank: Largest continent
Highest point: Mount Everest (Himalayas), over 29,000 ft.
Lowest point: Dead Sea, 1349 feet below sea level
Main languages: Arabic, Chinese, English, and Russian
Largest country: Russia
Smallest country: Maldives
World's largest inland body of water: Caspian Sea
Main rivers: Yangtze, Huang, and Xi in China; Euphrates and Tigris in Turkey and Iraq
Longest river: Yangtze (3900 miles)

Asia

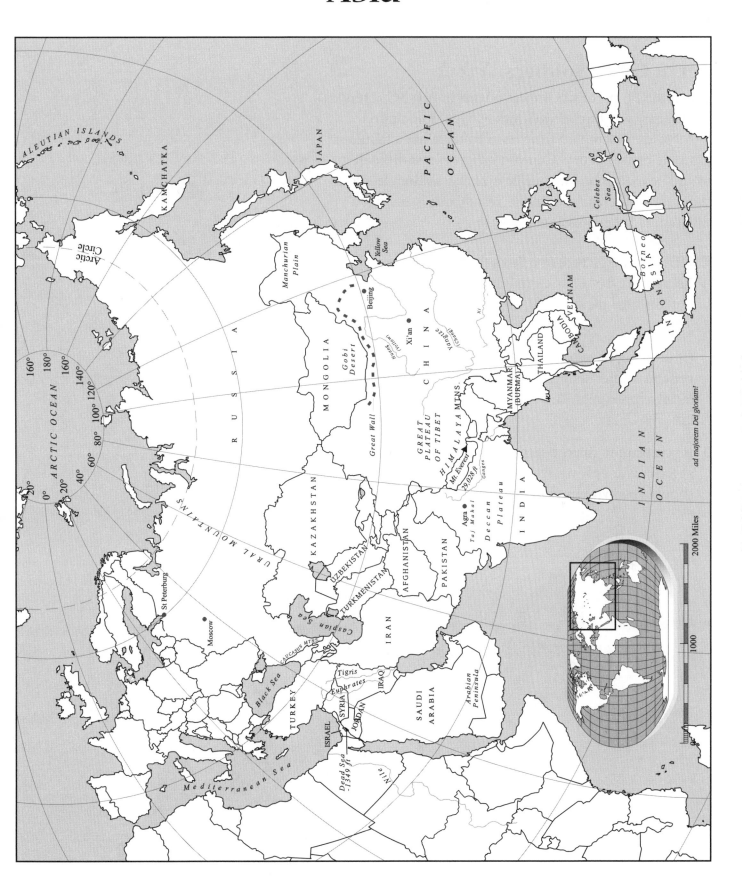

GEOGRAPHY THROUGH ART

CHINA 🍴

Terra Cotta Soldiers ☆☆☆　ⓘ

When the Emperor of Qin was buried in 210 BC, a replica of his army was buried with him at Xian. It included 8,099 soldiers sculpted from terra cotta. What a fabulous example of art history! Can you imagine how difficult it would be to even make one life-size clay soldier, let alone thousands? Each soldier in the Terra Cotta army has a different facial expression.

Materials
paper
pencils
modeling clay

1. First, draw a picture of a Terra Cotta soldier. Remember from our earth lesson that this is a one-dimensional piece of art.

2. Next, try to sculpt a soldier using your modeling clay. (It does not have to be life size!) Start by making a general soldier shape, then add details like armor and facial expressions. This is a three-dimensional piece of art.

3. If you want to make a terra cotta army like the soldiers at Xian, you only need to make 8,098 more soldiers. This should keep you busy for a while!

QuickSketch: Pagoda

The pagoda is a famous style of Chinese building. The style was imported from India. Most pagodas were originally used to store sacred Buddhist relics. There are many forms of pagodas, differing from one region of the country to the next. They all have a few things in common, including an odd number of levels and upturned roof eaves. The roofs were curved because the Chinese people believed curves repelled evil spirits, who they thought liked to lurk around straight lines. Draw a pagoda in your geography notebook, tracing the picture if necessary to help get you started.

Tangram Puzzle ☆☆

Tangram is an ancient Chinese puzzle. It is essentially a square divided into seven different pieces. The pieces are then put together to form a picture. The picture must use all seven shapes, which must be touching but not overlapping.

Materials
tracing paper
pencil
cardstock or cardboard
glue
colored pencils or markers

1. Trace the outline of the tangram on this page onto your tracing paper.

2. Glue the paper to a sheet of cardstock. (For a sturdier tangram, glue to cardboard.) Cut along the lines.

3. You can leave your tangram plain or decorate it as desired with pencils or markers.

4. Use your pieces to create a figure of your choice, following the rules listed in the introduction. You could make a person, dog, cat, bird, rabbit, etc.

5. If you come up with a design you really like, trace it onto a sheet of paper. You can then color the design and add a background. You could even include multiple figures in the same piece of art.

6. Save your tangram pieces in a sandwich bag.

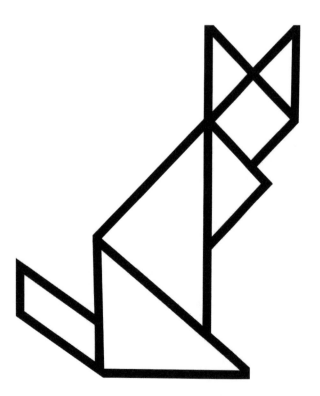

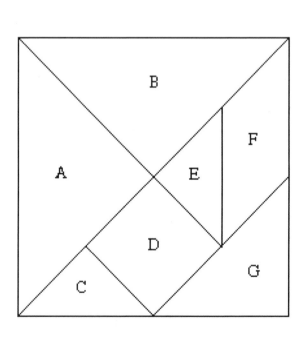

Chinese Paper Cutting

The creation of paper as we know it is largely attributed to the ancient Chinese people. Cai Lun, a court official, invented a paper made from wood pulp about 100 AD. Because it was not mass-produced, only the wealthiest Chinese, usually from the royal family, could afford paper for crafting beautiful paper cuttings. Eventually, paper became more affordable and all classes of society began to place emphasis on the art of paper cutting. In fact, a woman's worth as a bride was often based on how beautiful and intricate her

cuttings were. Paper cutting still remains a very important folk art. At festival times, cut paper designs are not only sold in the streets, but are also given as gifts and greetings. The cuttings usually include a traditional Chinese animal, such as a panda, dragon, or tiger. They are often hung in a window or door so that the sunlight accents the cuts. Paper cuts are done in many different colors, but the most traditional color is red because it represents good luck and success in the Chinese culture.

Materials
scissors
red paper
pencil
hole punch
gold ribbon

Paper Cutting

You can try your hand at paper cutting. Simply follow the instructions below.

1. Draw a design on the paper of a panda, dragon, or tiger. You can trace one of the images provided in the Appendix if you want.

2. Cut out the design along the lines you have drawn.

3. Put a hole in the top of your design using the hole punch. Put a length of gold ribbon through the hole and tie.

4. Hang your paper cut in a window or on the wall.

Culture Connection: SNOWFLAKES

Have you ever cut out a paper snowflake to decorate your house during the winter? Then you have done your own version of a Chinese paper cutting. Paper snowflakes can be hung in a window just like Chinese paper cuttings. They can also be used to decorate Christmas cards or even as gift tags. This winter, try to add some different shapes and designs to your snowflakes with what you have learned in this lesson.

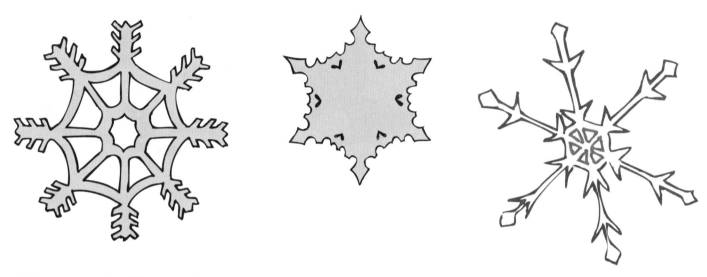

Chinese Calligraphy

There are several ways that writing in China is different from writing we may be familiar with. First, instead of having letters of the alphabet that are put together to form words, the Chinese have characters that represent whole words. Sometimes these characters are combined with other characters to create new words as well. Second, some Chinese characters were originally **pictographs**, meaning they were actually pictures symbolizing the word they describe. You can still recognize some characters because they resemble the word they represent. Lastly, writing in China is considered an art, equal in prestige to other arts such as painting or drawing. It is usually done with a brush using black ink. Even though there are thousands of Chinese characters, there are only eight basic brush strokes used to make the characters. Students of calligraphy study for years to perfect the art of writing. ⓘ

| Spring | Summer | Autumn | Winter |

QUICKSKETCH: GREAT WALL OF CHINA

The Great Wall of China is the longest man-made structure on earth. It is actually a series of walls and forts built and maintained over centuries of China's existence. It was built to keep out invaders from the north. Can you imagine having a wall built around your city that you could drive a car on? How about a wall around your entire state? Or across the whole country? Now you get the idea, because the Great Wall is over 4,000 miles long. Look at the picture of the Great Wall on this page. Try to draw a similar one in your geography notebook. Notice how the wall looks large in the foreground and very small in the background. Draw a picture of yourself in the front of the picture, standing on the Great Wall. Now draw a picture of yourself in the background. Did you change the size of your body so that the picture looks realistic? You should be larger in the front of the picture, and smaller in the back. In real life, things look smaller the farther away they are.

Culture Connection: HIEROGLYPHICS

What is another language we have learned about that utilized pictographs? What about ancient Egypt? The ancient Egyptians also used pictures in the form of hieroglyphics. Turn to the section on hieroglyphics for more information.

Seals - Identifying Marks

As you look at art from China online or in a library book, you may notice that the surface of the work contains red markings. There may be one or two, or the entire background may be covered with these markings, called **seals**. Seals are identifying marks placed on the painting by either the artist or owner of the work. This reflects a difference in culture between Western and Eastern countries. Can you imagine what we would think if every owner of the Mona Lisa had signed their name somewhere on the painting? This would definitely lower its value! In China, however, there is pride found in the seals because they link the current owner to all the past owners of the piece.

Materials
large rubber erasers
pencil
a sharp knife
a red ink pad for stamping

Chinese Seals ☆☆

1. Design a seal for yourself on paper. You can include your full name, or just your initials. You might also like to include some symbols that show what you are interested in. Keep the design simple. Intricate details won't show up well when you are stamping.

2. When you are happy with your seal, draw it with your pencil on one of the erasers. Make your lines extra thick and bold.

3. Have an adult cut along the outside of your lines with the knife. Wipe away any excess rubber pieces.

4. Press your seal firmly onto a red ink pad. Stamp onto your artwork. You might try making several seals with different symbols for different kinds of art.

Note: Remember that stamps print a mirror image. Any letters or numbers will need to be written backwards to stamp correctly.

QUICKSKETCH: DRAGON

When we think of China, we often think of dragons. Was the creature that the Chinese call a dragon really an extinct dinosaur? Many people believe that it was. There have been more dinosaur egg fossils found in China than anywhere in the world.

The Chinese people had at least three words for dragon. Each word meant a dragon with a different number of toes—three, four, or five. In your geography notebook, draw your dragon with however many toes you choose. ⓘ

Chinese Scrolls ☆☆

Creating a Chinese scroll is a fun and different way to display your art. Landscapes are a very popular subject for scroll painting in China. You will often see sweeping panoramas of mountain ranges or close-up views of troubled ocean waters. If there are any people present in the landscapes, they are usually quite small compared to the nature surrounding them. This is because the ancient Chinese believed that nature was more powerful and awe-inspiring than the human race. The landscapes are often accompanied by short poems about nature.

Materials
a picture of a landscape
painting paper
watercolors
markers
glue
yarn or ribbon

1. Study the landscape picture for inspiration. You may use any picture of a nature scene, or use a Chinese landscape. You might even try the view out of a window at your house.

2. It may help you to sketch the landscape a few times on scrap paper to get a feel for what you want to paint.

3. Start with the outline of the landscape using black watercolor. You can paint your picture either horizontally or vertically. Then fill in with colors. Be sure to paint from edge to edge on the paper. Dry thoroughly.

4. Write a short poem about what is in your picture. Using a marker, write it in the background of your painting.

5. If desired, turn to the section on Maps to learn how to age the scroll painting. You might also wish to add a red seal (see the project Chinese Seals) to your painting.

6. Roll up each edge of the watercolor and glue with white glue. It will help if you hold the ends together with paperclips. Alternately, you may wish to glue the painting to a set of dowel rods.

7. Glue or tape a length of yarn or ribbon to the scroll for hanging.

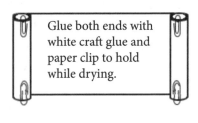

Glue both ends with white craft glue and paper clip to hold while drying.

QᴜɪᴄᴋSᴋᴇᴛᴄʜ: Hᴀʟʟ ᴏꜰ Pʀᴀʏᴇʀ ꜰᴏʀ Gᴏᴏᴅ Hᴀʀᴠᴇsᴛs

This beautiful building is located in Beijing at the Temple of Heaven. Can you see the intricate patterns on the walls of the building? This wooden building was originally built so that the emperor could go there to pray for good harvests for the land. The circular building is built on a marble base. As you sketch this photograph, pay close attention to the shading. In the photo, the building is darker on the right side than it is on the left. If you include this in your sketch, your building will look more realistic.

Photo Archives of Famous Places of the World by Donald Witte

Culture Connection: SILO

Do we ever see church buildings in the United States that are round like the Hall of Prayer for Good Harvests? Not usually, although there are a few. What is something we more commonly see that is made in a cylindrical design? If you live in the country, you probably are thinking of a farm silo. The farm silo is a great example of a building made in the form a cylinder. Silos were originally built as squares or rectangles. However, air pockets often formed in the corners of the building, causing the grain to spoil. Silos were then built as cylinders to solve this problem. As an added benefit, the new silos could withstand much stronger wind gusts than the old ones. ⓘ

Hmong Story Cloth ☆☆☆

The Hmong people are originally from China. Over time, however, they have dispersed and now reside all over Southeast Asia including the countries of Cambodia, Laos, Burma, and Vietnam. For many years, the Hmong had no written language, so all information was transmitted orally, including folk tales and legends. Now the Hmong people retell these legends on pieces of cloth, which are often used as decorative wall hangings. Each piece is full of small details and many different scenes of the story. To get an idea or the beauty and intricacy of these cloths, search online or visit your local library.

Materials
**1-yard plain colored fabric
(muslin works well)
fabric crayons
fabric paint
needle & thread
buttons, ribbons, sequins,
& other trinkets**

1. Select a story for your story cloth. You can use a favorite book, fairytale, or even a movie.

2. Decide what scenes you want to include. Include enough to give a good overview of the story.

3. It may help to begin by sketching your scenes on another sheet of paper. Then decorate the cloth using fabric paint and crayons. You may want to decorate your cloth with buttons, ribbons, or embroidery.

☆ Primary students can make a story cloth on poster board.

☆☆ Intermediate students should have an adult help with any sewing that may need to be done. Ask an adult to hem the edges of your cloth to keep it intact.

Photo courtesy of Masami Suga of her family Hmong story cloth

Culture Connection: MOVIE STORYBOARDS

While we may have never seen a Hmong story cloth, we have probably heard of a movie **storyboard**. A storyboard is one of the first steps in making a movie. A moviemaker will take the movie plot and have an artist draw out each scene. This is used as the basis for the real scenes in the movie. This makes planning the movie locations, props, and crew requirements much easier because it has already been done on paper.

INDIA 🍴

Miniature Painting ☆☆ ⓘ

Miniature paintings were an important part of Indian art starting with the Mughal dynasty. These paintings were usually not displayed on the wall in frames but were bound together like books. Many emperors commissioned the production of such books, particularly Emperor Akbar in the 16th century. Artists were often brought over from neighboring Persia to work on these exquisite pieces. Many different genres were included in the miniature paintings, including portraits, landscapes, and even paintings that told stories. Sometimes pages of calligraphy were also bound into the books. The paintings were usually watercolors with an opaque, rather than transparent, finish. Tiny brushes were used to detail the pictures, which also had intricate borders. Metallic accents were often added to enhance a painting's beauty.

Materials

light-colored cardstock
scissors
pencils
watercolors
small paintbrushes
metallic gel pens
metallic paint
hole punch
ribbon
stapler

1. Trim the cardstock to a small size, anywhere from 3" by 3" to 5" by 5".

2. Lightly sketch an image of what you want to paint. Remember that you can paint people, animals, nature, or any subject that interests you.

3. Paint a miniature using watercolors.

4. When the painting has thoroughly dried, use gel pens or paint in gold, silver, or copper to accent your piece.

5. If you wish, paint several miniatures. You can then bind them together by punching holes and tying them together with ribbon or simply by stapling them together.

Batik ☆☆☆ ⓘ

Batik is art done on fabric. It is created by applying a resistant substance, such as hot wax, and then dyeing the fabric. The wax prevents the dye from covering the entire fabric. When the wax is removed, it leaves a negative space in the picture. (For more on positive and negative space, see the lesson Earth from Space.)

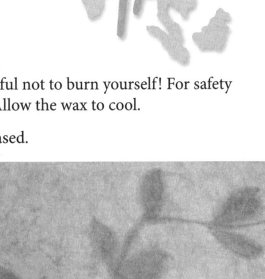

Materials
plain 100% cotton fabric
paraffin wax
small paintbrush
cookie cutters or stencils
cold water fabric dye

1. Trim the fabric to the size you desire. You can make it the size of a pillow, wall hanging, or even a scarf. Keep in mind what you want your finished project to be.

2. Have an adult heat the wax on the stove until it is thoroughly melted.

3. Using cookie cutters or stencils as a guide, paint multiple designs on the fabric using the hot wax. Be very careful not to burn yourself! For safety purposes, wear gloves while handling the wax or fabric dye. Allow the wax to cool.

4. Dye the fabric following the directions for the dye you purchased.

5. When the fabric has thoroughly dried, you can remove the wax. The best way to do this is to iron it with a warm iron. Place several layers of newspaper on both sides of the fabric, then iron. (The newspaper will help absorb the wax and keep it from getting on your iron.)

6. You can repeat the steps again to create a multi-layered look. (Start with the lightest color dye you will be using and work to the darkest color.)

Note: Paraffin wax can usually be purchased in the canning section of your local grocery store. You can also find it in the candle making section of any **craft** or hobby store.

Photo by Joan Brightman

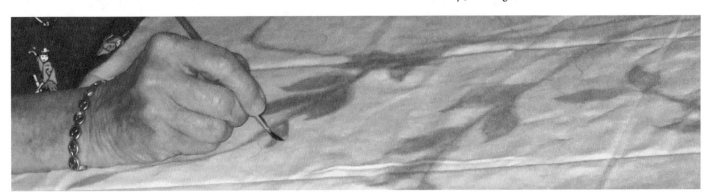

Photo by Kim Whitmore-Weber

Easy Batik ☆

Here is an easier version of batik for younger students.

1. Color a design on the paper using crayons. (Do not use the color black.) Bold, bright designs work best. Be sure to cover every inch of the paper.

2. When you are done coloring your picture, soak it in water. Crumple the paper into a ball.

3. Unroll the crumpled paper. Paint a thin layer of black poster paint over the wet picture.

4. Let dry. The effects will resemble the much more complicated fabric batik!

Materials
crayons
construction paper
water
black poster paint

QUICKSKETCH: ELEPHANT

In India, some people worship the elephant as a god. Using your encyclopedia, look up why an African elephant is different than an Indian elephant. In your geography notebook, draw a picture of an Indian elephant in its natural habitat. Use the sketches on the left as a guide for how the elephant should be drawn. Be sure to erase any extra pencil marks when you are done.

Taj Mahal ☆

The Taj Mahal, located in Agra, India, is the most famous mausoleum in Islamic architecture. Built by the Shah Jahan for his favorite wife, it was completed around 1648. The building, made of white marble, has since become famous all over the world. There is a reflecting pool in front of the building that we will mimic in our watercolor.

1. Draw a rough sketch of the Taj Mahal on the top half of the paper.

2. Paint your sketch using watercolors. Let dry thoroughly.

3. Using a clean brush, brush water onto the bottom half of the paper until it is just damp.

4. Fold the paper in half, pressing the top onto the bottom.

5. Unfold the paper. You should have a likeness of the Taj Mahal in the reflecting pool on the bottom of the paper.

Materials
watercolor paper
pencils
watercolors
paintbrushes

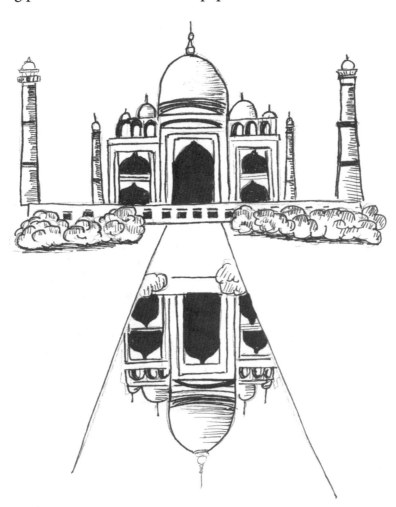

JAPAN

Fish Printing ☆

Gyotaku, the Japanese art of making fish prints, began about one hundred years ago. Most fishermen in Japan sell their catches to make money for their families, so gyotaku is a way to record their biggest and best catches and still be able to sell the fish. The prints are often hung on the wall, much like we might see a fish mounted by a taxidermist. The prints are sometimes kept in a journal, so a man's fishing record is all neatly kept in one place.

If you prefer not to use a real fish, do a quick search online for gyotaku rubber fish to find fake fish for printing. You could also use other things in nature, such as rocks, leaves, or flowers.

1. If you are using a real fish, rinse the fish with vinegar to remove any dirt or slimy residue. Pat dry with paper towels.

2. Select a paint color to use for the fish print. Prints were originally done with blue ink, so blue would be the most traditional. Now, however, all colors are used, often with multiple colors on the same print.

3. Using your paintbrush, paint the color onto the fish being careful to cover every part. You do not have to worry about painting the eye since it does not hold paint well. (This is a great time to study the different parts of the fish.) ⓘ

4. Press the tissue paper firmly onto the fish. Once the paper has touched the fish, be careful not to move it! This will help you avoid smudges.

5. Allow the print to dry. Sign your name to the print. If you made a print of a fish you caught yourself, be sure to put the date, time, and location that you caught the fish. You may wish to frame your print to avoid tearing the tissue paper.

Materials
one small dead fish, fresh or frozen
vinegar
paper towels
paintbrush
poster paint
white tissue paper

Sumi-e Ink Painting ☆☆ ⓘ

Japanese ink painting started in China during the time 1336-1573. Japanese monks traveled to China to learn the ink painting styles of Zen. Today this is considered an important art in many Asian countries. In **sumi-e**, the important thing is to capture the essence of something in as few strokes as possible. The resulting product is simple, yet beautiful. It is characterized by basic lines and dots in various tones of black. Sometimes, the drawing will be colored with paints, but the black lines must always be visible.

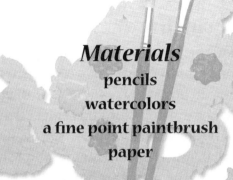

Materials
pencils
watercolors
a fine point paintbrush
paper

1. Pick a subject for your painting. It will help to have a picture of your subject nearby for study. Look at it closely. Focus on the main lines, the essence of it.

2. Quickly sketch your subject on scrap paper. Look closely at the sketch to see what lines are not necessary or what lines could be added to better illustrate the subject. Don't worry about small details.

3. Sketch it a few more times to be sure you have exactly the look you want.

4. On a fresh sheet of paper, paint your subject using black paint. Use your sketch as a reference.

5. When the painting has dried, add some accent colors if desired.

Sumi-e paintings courtesy of Joan Lok.

Sumi-e paintings courtesy of Carla Jaranson.

Culture Connection: CARICATURES

Much like sumi-e, a **caricature** strives to capture the essence of a person rather than an exact replica of their likeness. These are usually quick sketches done for humorous effect, exaggerating a person's most noticeable features. At first glance, a caricature should be easily recognizable as the person it represents. When you are done with your sumi-e painting, try a caricature of yourself or a friend.

The Legend of Sumi-e

There is a legend of an ancient Chinese emperor who commissioned an artist to paint a sumi-e picture of a chicken, the emperor's favorite animal. The artist went to live with the chickens. For over a year he ate, slept, and watched the chickens very closely, but he never painted any chickens. The Emperor grew increasingly angry. He was paying the artist to paint pictures of chickens, not to live like a chicken! Finally, the emperor had the artist brought to him. He demanded to see his art or he would behead him. The artist sat down and in a brief moment painted his first chicken. The Emperor was astounded, because it was the best picture he had ever seen of a chicken. With just a few brush strokes, the artist had captured the essence of a chicken. He became the chief artist of the land.

Origami ☆☆

Origami is the art of paper folding. It is a traditional Japanese pastime that has become popular all over the world. Much like Chinese paper cutting, in the past only the very wealthy could afford paper for folding. Now anyone can enjoy this hobby. Almost any form you can imagine can be folded in origami. You usually start with a square sheet of paper. Follow the steps in the illustrations below to create your own origami frog. You can color it with markers or pencils if desired when you are done folding.

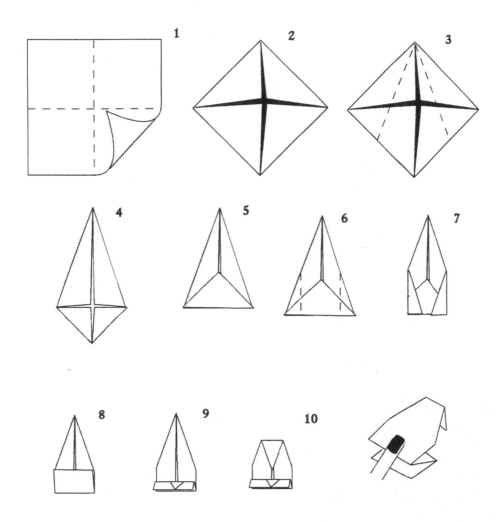

Divider Screen ☆☆

Japanese divider screens are a very old art that are sometimes seen in houses as decorations today. They are used to divide a larger room into smaller sections. In this project, we will make a miniature version of the divider screen.

Materials
18″ by 11″ foam board
pencil
razor blade
pencils
poster paint
markers

1. You will need to divide the foam-board panel into three folding pieces. It will be best to have an adult help with this. Using a pencil, divide the panel into three equal portions. Have the adult cut the panels with a razor blade where you have marked, going only halfway through the foam.

2. Using a pencil, lightly sketch what you want to paint on both sides of the divider screen.

3. When you are satisfied with your drawings, paint the divider screen, being sure to cover every part of the surface. The creases where you have cut the board should be painted black.

Hina Matsuri

A favorite festival for girls in Japan is Hina Matsuri, or Girl's Day. It is held every year on March 3rd. At this festival, mothers hand down dolls to their daughters, repeating a tradition passed down from generation to generation. These dolls are displayed in a special way on the day of the festival. A series of steps are covered with red fabric. On the top shelf are dolls representing the emperor and empress. On the next shelf are all the members of the court. On the third shelf are the court's musicians. The last shelf usually contains other miniature items that might be needed by the dolls, such as furniture. Cake, candy, and drinks are served at the celebration. At the end of the day, all of the dolls are carefully put away until next year.

Materials
paper
pencils
modeling clay

Girl's Day Dolls ✰✰✰

1. Pick a favorite character from a book or story to use for your doll. You can also choose to design your own doll not based on another character.

2. Draw the doll on paper. What facial features will your doll have? What kind of outfit will it wear?

3. If you choose, you can sculpt your doll out of modeling clay.

Culture Connection: CHRISTMAS ORNAMENTS

Only the Japanese usually celebrate Hina Matsuri, but can you think of a similar holiday in our own culture? Christmas is somewhat like it. Although we leave our decorations out for more than one day, we do usually put them away at a specified time. What specific Christmas traditions does your family have? Are there any other special holidays where your family brings out special things? Consider coming up with a new holiday to start your own tradition!

Kodomo no hi

Kodomo no hi is the boy's equivalent to Hina Matsuri in Japan. It is a centuries-old Japanese tradition that celebrates boys. It takes place on the fifth of May every year. At this time, families with boys hang koinobori from flagpoles in their yard. Koinobori is a fish-shaped banner. Each male in the family is represented by a koinobori on the flagpole. The largest one, at the top, represents the father, and then each son from oldest to youngest.

Boy's Day Fish Banners ☆

1. Cut along the outside of the template. If you desire to make a larger banner, you can make your own version of the template on a large sheet of paper, such as banner paper or brown wrapping paper.

2. Color the carp with bright colors using either the markers or poster paint. When you are done, fold it in half along the dotted line.

3. Staple the fish together along its belly, leaving the ends unstapled. Punch a hole through both sides near the eye. Run the desired length of string through the hole and fasten to the dowel rod. Staple streamers to the end of the fish as a tail. You are now ready to fly your koinobori!

Materials
a copy of the carp template
(from the Appendix)
poster board
pictures of fish
scissors
markers
poster paint
stapler
hole punch
streamers
string
dowel rod

Culture Connection: KOI

A very special creature in Japan is the Koi. It is a type of carp that the Japanese breed because they believe they are beautiful, intelligent, and friendly. They also believe they bring good luck. A Koi often looks like an extra large, extremely beautiful goldfish. You can probably see one at your local pet store. Although we might not think there is anything special about this kind of fish, the Japanese people hold them in high esteem. Do we in America have an animal that we think is special? Perhaps our national symbol, the eagle? What about your state? If you don't know, find out what your state bird, animal, or fish is.

Folded Fan ☆

Fans have been used around the world for thousands of years as a way to cool off in warm temperatures, but it was not until the eighth century that the Japanese invented the folding fan. Since that time, it has become an important part of Japanese culture. Fans were used in dances, as weapons, and as advertisements. They were sometimes painted and sometimes made of cut paper designs.

Materials
white construction paper
pencils
watercolors
paintbrushes
glitter
popsicle sticks
poster paint
school glue

1. Choose a theme for your fan. Japanese fans were often painted with landscapes or dragons. Sketch a rough outline of your design on the paper.

2. Paint your design using the watercolors. Accent important parts of the design with glitter.

3. Paint the popsicle sticks black or gold with the poster paint. Let dry.

4. Fold the fan and glue painted popsicle sticks to each end. You are now ready to use your fan or hang it for display.

RUSSIA 🍴

Russian Mosaics ☆

The Church of the Resurrection of Christ is located in St. Petersburg, Russia. It was built on the exact spot where Alexander II was assassinated in March 1881. His son had the church built in his memory. The church is decorated inside and out with unique mosaics, designed by some of the most prominent Russian artists of the day. The mosaics depict many religious events, including a comparison of Alexander's assassination to the death of Jesus Christ.

Materials
different colors of paper
pencils
white cardstock
glue

1. Draw a picture on cardstock of what you want your mosaic to look like. Large shapes work better than smaller ones. Remember that mosaics in the Church of the Resurrection of Christ were often images of Bible stories or religious symbols.

2. Tear colored paper into small pieces.

3. Glue the paper onto your cardstock design. You can use all of one color for each shape, or mix the colors within the shapes.

☆☆ Intermediate or Secondary students may wish to use scissors to cut up their paper rather than tearing it.

Culture Connection: BUTTERFLY WING ART

A mosaic is a piece of art composed of many different colored tiles or glass. These pieces of tile or glass are all pieces of the bigger picture. This is like the Butterfly Wing Art that we learned about in Africa. While similar to those collages, the Russian mosaics are different because they are usually pictures of religious figures or events. The African collages generally depict scenes of nature or everyday people.

Photo Archives of Famous Places of the World by Donald Witte

Matryoshka Doll ☆ ⓘ

A Russian Matryoshka doll, sometimes called a nesting doll, is a special treasure. If you have ever had the privilege of seeing one, you know how charming these little dolls are. The dolls are usually painted in bright colors and each doll is smaller that the last, so they fit inside of each other perfectly. We will make an easy cone version of the dolls.

Materials
construction paper or cardstock
matryoshka doll template
(from the Appendix)
scissors
glue
markers

1. Trace the shapes from the doll template onto a piece of construction paper or cardstock. (If desired, you can copy the shapes directly onto the cardstock with a copying machine.)

2. Cut out shapes from the paper. Fold the shapes to form a cone. Place a line of glue along the glue line. Lay the other edge on the glued edge to fasten the cone together.

3. Decorate your dolls like the sample matryoshka dolls on this page. You can then stack them inside each other from smallest to largest!

Note: If you are interested in making real dolls instead of the cone version in this project, look for unpainted nesting dolls at your local craft or hobby store.

⌐Culture Connection: FOLK ART

Matryoshka dolls are Russian folk art. Folk art is art done by common people. It usually differs in style drastically from art done by trained artists. Matryoshka dolls were often painted by regular people and children, which resulted in a simple, unique style. The dolls were usually made from leftover scraps of wood.

Every country and culture has its own version of folk art. America, for example, has cornhusk dolls. Early American pioneers made the dolls from leftover pieces of dried cornhusks. The dolls were then used as toys by the children.

Materials
foam board
sharp pencil
black poster paint
paintbrush
white paper

Lubok ☆☆

Lubok is a form of Russian folk art. These prints were originally made from woodcuts.

1. Decide on the design you want for your lubok. Sketch the design on a piece of paper first to be sure you include everything you want. You may want to tell a short story with your picture. (Your print will be a mirror image. Be sure to put any numbers or letters backwards so they will print correctly.)

2. Have an adult cut the foam board so it is the same size as your paper.

3. Etch your design onto the foam board with your pencil. Be sure your marks are deep.

4. Paint the poster paint onto the foam board. Press the painted side of the board onto a fresh sheet of white paper. Gently lift the foam board from the paper. You now have your very own Russian Lubok!

Culture Connection: COMIC BOOKS

The art of lubok is often considered a precursor to the modern day comic strip. The prints often contained a series of pictures that were accompanied by short stories with morals. The stories, meant to make people laugh, were often sarcastic in nature. Because one woodcut could make many prints, lubki were available at affordable prices. Many Russian people might have the same print in their house, much like we might have the same comic strip hanging on our refrigerator.

QUICKSKETCH: REINDEER

Reindeer can be found in northern Russia. Images of reindeer are often found in Russian folk art, like the example on this page. In your geography notebook, draw an image of a reindeer. (You can even draw a folk art reindeer like the one you see here.) Beside it, draw a picture of a common American deer. You can use the picture and steps shown here as a reference. What things are similar between the two types of deer? What things are different? Make a list in your geography notebook. Use an encyclopedia to gather more information about these two types of deer for your list.

Reindeer

American deer

Russian Pins ☆

Russian pins are very beautiful. Years ago pins were hand-painted on paper mache. They were often painted black. Then a small still-life painting, such as flowers, fruits, or a cityscape, was painted onto the pin.

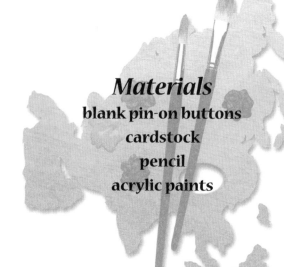

Materials
blank pin-on buttons
cardstock
pencil
acrylic paints

1. Cut out a piece of cardstock to fit inside the pin front. (You may want to cut a few extras in case you make a mistake.)

2. Lightly sketch the design you want to make onto your paper.

3. Paint your design. Let dry thoroughly before putting it inside your pin.

Note: Blank pin on buttons are available in most craft and hobby aisles of retail stores. They are sometimes called "memory buttons." If you cannot locate any, make your own by gluing a craft safety pin to the back of your design.

Culture Connection: MINIATURE PAINTINGS

What other project have we done that is similar to this? The Indian miniature paintings are also done on a very small scale. Locate India and Russia on a world map. How close together are the two countries? Is it possible that the idea of small paintings might have traveled from one country to the other?

AUSTRALIA

Continent Summary

The continent of Australia, including New Zealand and over 25,000 neighboring islands, makes up the region often called Oceania. It is a diverse land with a wide range of unique flora and fauna found nowhere else in the world. Because Australia is located in the Southern Hemisphere, spring begins in September and fall in March.

Besides being both the world's sixth largest country and the world's smallest continent, Australia also has a few other world records. It is the lowest, flattest, and driest continent in the world and home to Ayers Rock, the largest monolith in the world. This 2800+ foot high red sandstone landmark is located in central Australia's outback. Another "world's largest" located in Australia is The Great Barrier Reef. There are over 400 types of coral in this 1200-mile-long reef taking up an area of 80,000 square miles. An unbelievable variety of fish swims in the waters along the reef. Can you guess how many? Over 1500 kinds of fish!

Australia is surrounded by a number of seas, the Pacific Ocean and the Indian Ocean and is made up of three main physical regions. (1) The Great Western Plateau is a low semi-arid (fairly dry climate) land where scrubby grasses and spiky bushes are scattered among wide areas of sandy, pebbly soil. This barren, sparsely populated land is called the Outback, and it makes up two-thirds of the continent. You see few trees here but loads of sand. Sand dunes, sand hills, and sand ridges as high as 60 feet! (2) The Central Lowlands has an area where salty streams are formed from mountain runoff. This water is used primarily for irrigation, as it is too salty to drink. The best farmland is in the southeast where it gets its water from the Murray-Darling water system. (3) The Eastern Highlands (Great Dividing Range) divides the fertile coast from the central dry lands. This region has steep mountains used to generate hydroelectricity. Australia's highest mountain peak, Mt. Kosciusko (7310 ft. elevation) is located in the Eastern Highlands.

Australia's 33 countries and dependencies are divided into 6 states and 2 territories, but most of its citizens live at or near the coastline. Native Australians are called Aborigines. The most common languages spoken in Australia are English, local languages, some Japanese and French. The two main countries in this continent are Australia and New Zealand. The continent of Australia is a major world producer of wool, veal, and mutton. In New Zealand, sheep outnumber humans fourteen to one!

Facts
Size: smallest about 3,300,000 square miles
Rank: smallest continent
Highest point in Oceania: Mt. Wilhelm, Papua New Guinea, 14,800 ft.
Highest point in mainland Australia: Mt Kosciusko, 7310 ft.
Lowest point: Lake Eyre –38 ft. elevation
Main rivers: Murray-Darling system (Darling, Lachlan, Murray)
Largest country: Australia
Smallest country: Nauru
Main languages: English, local languages, some Japanese and French
Largest island: New Guinea (world's second largest)
Crops: wheat, barley, oats, fruit, sugarcane, livestock, wool
Agriculture and industry: bauxite, alumina, gold, silver, lead, zinc, copper, iron, tungsten, and coal

Oceania

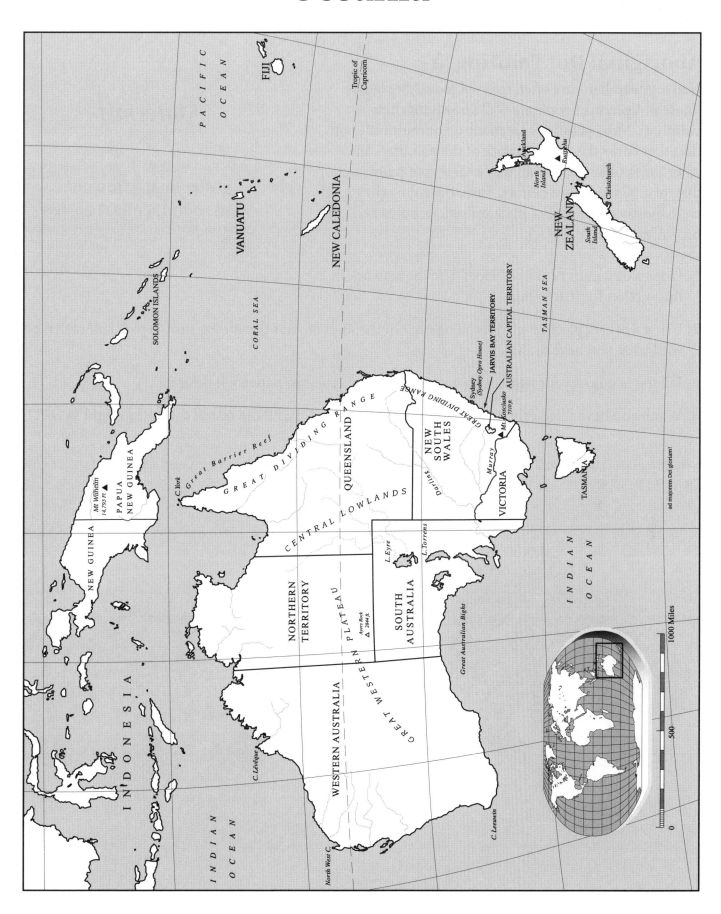

PACIFIC OCEAN

FIJI

Tropic of Capricorn

VANUATU

NEW CALEDONIA

Auckland
Ruapehu
North Island
NEW ZEALAND
Christchurch
South Island

SOLOMON ISLANDS

CORAL SEA

TASMAN SEA

GREAT DIVIDING RANGE

Sydney (Sydney Opra House)
JARVIS BAY TERRITORY
AUSTRALIAN CAPITAL TERRITORY
Mt. Kosciusko 7310 ft.

ad majorem Dei gloriam!

Mt Wilhelm 14,793 Ft.

PAPUA NEW GUINEA

Great Barrier Reef

C. York

GREAT DIVIDING RANGE

QUEENSLAND

NEW SOUTH WALES

Darling
Murray
VICTORIA

NEW GUINEA

CENTRAL LOWLANDS

L. Eyre
L. Torrens

TASMANIA

INDONESIA

NORTHERN TERRITORY

PLATEAU
Ayers Rock 2844 ft.

SOUTH AUSTRALIA

INDIAN OCEAN

C. Lévêque

GREAT WESTERN

Great Australian Bight

1000 Miles

WESTERN AUSTRALIA

500

INDIAN OCEAN

North West C.

C. Leeuwin

0

GEOGRAPHY THROUGH ART

AUSTRALIA

Aboriginal Dot Painting ☆

Native Australians are often referred to as Aborigines. These indigenous people are well known for their paintings. Most paintings are made up of multitudes of dots that cover the entire surface of the painting. The Aborigines of ancient times made their own paints out of dirt, plants, seeds, and berries. Thus, the colors they used were mostly earth tones—mustard yellow, burnt red, dirt brown, and charcoal black.

Materials
paper
pencil
poster or acrylic paint
small, round sponge brushes

1. Draw a design in pencil on paper. Use the artwork in this section for inspiration.

2. Using a brush, place small dots along each of the lines of your design. Be sure to pick colors that go with what you have drawn.

3. Fill the inside of your figure with dots in a different color or pattern, if desired.

4. When you have filled everything you have drawn with dots, fill the rest of the background as well.

Note: If you do not have a small, round sponge brush, try to find something else with a round tip. A cotton swab could work, or even the tip of your pinky finger.

Aboriginal Stone Painting ☆

Aborigines often painted on the walls of the caves where they lived. Many art historians consider cave painting the beginning of art as we know it today. The Aborigines painted on the cave walls simple, outlines figures that represented their dreams. In this project, you will make your own stone painting.

Materials
smooth, flat rocks
pencil
acrylic or poster paint
varnish
paintbrush

1. Draw a design in pencil on the rock. Use the pictures on this page for inspiration.

2. Paint your design. Use earth tones like the Aborigines would have used.

3. Have an adult seal the rock painting with varnish. Let dry.

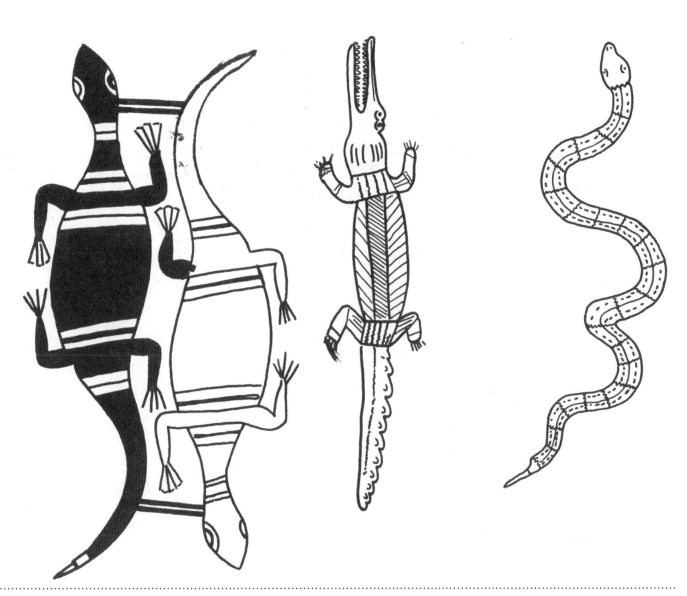

Aboriginal Bark Painting ☆

While the Aborigines started painting on stones, they were soon using other mediums. Eventually, they started doing their paintings on pieces of bark. The tree bark they used was reddish in color. Designs were usually painted in white. In this project, you will make a bark painting of your own.

Materials
brown craft paper
scissors
red watercolor
paintbrush
white chalk

1. Cut the craft paper to the size you choose for your completed work.

2. Paint the entire surface of the paper with red watercolor. Let dry.

3. Draw an aboriginal design on the paper with the white chalk. Animals were the most frequent subjects for paintings. Remember to keep the forms simple.

QuickSketch: Kangaroo

The kangaroo is a marsupial that is commonly found in Australia. As a marsupial, the female kangaroo has a pouch on the front. A baby kangaroo stays in this special pouch after it is born while it completes its development. A kangaroo has a large tail and stands on its two hind legs. It can hop up to forty miles an hour, but usually travels around ten or fifteen miles per hour. In your geography notebook, draw a kangaroo.

Didgeridoo ☆

A didgeridoo is a wind instrument first created and played by the Aborigines in Australia. It is usually a piece of Eucalyptus wood that has been naturally hollowed out by termites, although in modern times it is made with a wide variety of wood and even plastic. Here is an easy didgeridoo for you to make!

Materials
empty wrapping paper roll
markers

1. Draw a design on the wrapping paper roll. Be sure to use the aboriginal art in this section to help give you inspiration. Color the entire roll.

2. Hold the roll in your hands, with the bottom pointing towards the floor. Blow into the top to hear the noise!

Spiny Anteater ☆☆

Have you ever heard of an echidna? An echidna is sometimes called a spiny anteater. It is a member of the monotreme family, along with the duck-billed platypus. It looks like a mix between a porcupine and a regular anteater. For this project, make your own spiny anteater.

Materials
air-dry modeling clay
toothpicks
acrylic paints
paintbrush

1. Look at the picture on this page of a spiny anteater. Mold the clay into a similar shape. It should resemble a teardrop with a long, pointy end (the nose).

2. Put toothpicks all around the back of the anteater, as in the picture. These are the spikes!

3. Let the echidna thoroughly dry.

4. Paint your echidna.

QuickSketch: Sydney Opera House

The Sydney Opera House is one of the most famous performing arts centers in the world. There are four main auditoriums and nearly a thousand rooms encased in the interesting shell-shaped exterior. The building itself covers nearly five acres. Draw a picture of the Sydney Opera House in your geography notebook.

The Boomerang ☆☆

You've probably heard of a boomerang. While other ancient cultures used items similar to the boomerang, no culture used such advanced and varied versions as the Australian Aborigines. The boomerang, usually made of wood, was used for hunting, fighting, and just good, plain fun.

1. Using the template, trace the outline of the boomerangs marked 1, 2, and 3 onto a sheet of paper.

2. Glue the paper onto a piece of cardboard. Let dry.

3. Cut out the cardboard boomerangs.

4. Number 1 is the base or bottom layer. Glue number 2 onto the base in the place marked by the dotted line.

5. Glue number 3 onto the second piece in the space marked with the dotted line on the base. Let dry.

6. Notice the traditional animal designs from Australia. Put some designs on your boomerang with markers or tempera paint to decorate your flying machine.

Materials
boomerang template
(from the Appendix)
tracing paper
pencil
glue
cardboard
scissors
markers

Throwing a Boomerang

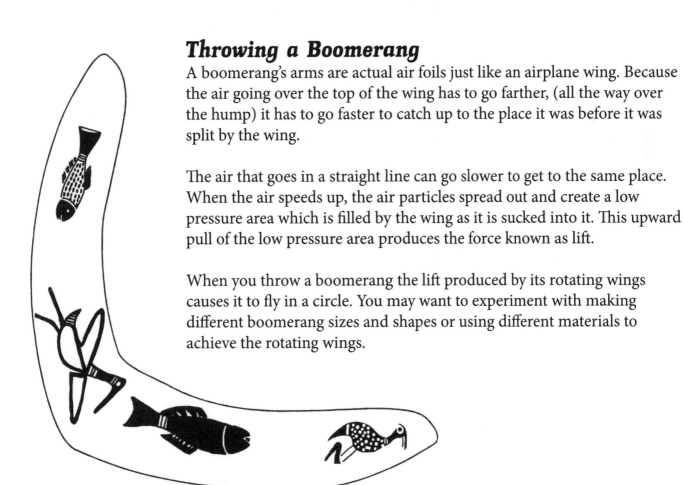

A boomerang's arms are actual air foils just like an airplane wing. Because the air going over the top of the wing has to go farther, (all the way over the hump) it has to go faster to catch up to the place it was before it was split by the wing.

The air that goes in a straight line can go slower to get to the same place. When the air speeds up, the air particles spread out and create a low pressure area which is filled by the wing as it is sucked into it. This upward pull of the low pressure area produces the force known as lift.

When you throw a boomerang the lift produced by its rotating wings causes it to fly in a circle. You may want to experiment with making different boomerang sizes and shapes or using different materials to achieve the rotating wings.

EUROPE

Continent Summary

Europe is the 2nd smallest continent in the world. Its eastern boundary is the Ural Mountains, which provide the dividing point of Europe and Asia. Europe's other boundaries include the Caspian Sea, Red Sea, Ural River, and Dardanelles Straits. Russia's land is in both Asia and Europe.

Europe is a mountainous land with plains in the central and eastern part of Europe and in France. The Scandinavian countries in the north are known for their fjords. The most well known mountains in Europe are probably the Swiss Alps. The Alps actually run through France, Italy, and Austria. Other mountain ranges include; the Carpathians in Romania, Slovakia, and Poland; Pyrenees between Spain and France; Apennine Mountains in Italy; Sudetic Mountains in Poland and the Czech Republic; and Transylvanian Alps in Romania.

The main rivers in Europe include: Volga, Danube, Rhone, and Rhine. Can you name the other main bodies of water in and around Europe? They are the Atlantic Ocean, Arctic Ocean, Mediterranean Sea, Black Sea, Norwegian Sea, and North Sea. Have you ever heard of the Chunnel? It is the nickname for the Channel Tunnel, a 31-mile-long train tunnel that runs under the English Channel. Although the United Kingdom is in Europe, it is surrounded by water and therefore separated from continental Europe. The Chunnel, completed in 1994, provides rail transportation between the UK and France where freight and passenger trains travel up to 100 miles per hour!

The culture of Europe is diverse, as are the number of languages spoken there. There are too many languages in Europe to list here, but the four main languages are English, French, German, and Russian. Although the many countries of Europe have each traditionally had their own currency, the Euro, a European currency, was introduced in 1999 with 9 countries participating. It is expected that more European countries will join the European Union as it proves to be successful. European farmers raise grain and livestock, and miners mine coal and iron ore. Fishing is a strong trade along the coasts of the Atlantic Ocean, Mediterranean Sea, and Black Sea.

The climate is generally humid except in the Mediterranean region where they have hot dry summers and cool wet winters. There are temperature extremes in Central and Eastern Europe where the climate is semi-arid to wet. The coldest part of Europe is above the Arctic Circle. Four countries in Europe have land within the Arctic Circle. They are Finland, Norway, Russia, and Sweden.

One of the most interesting cities in Europe is built on 118 islands on foundations of wooden pilings driven into the floor of the Adriatic Sea. Most of these islands are separated only by narrow canals. Transportation is provided by gondolas, ferries, and motor boats. This city is known for its beautiful buildings of Byzantine, Gothic, Greek, and Oriental architecture and its wonderful art museums. Do you know what city it is? Venice, Italy.

Facts
Size: 3,850,000 square miles
Rank: 2nd smallest continent
Highest point: Mount Elbrus, Russia 18,466 ft.
Lowest point: Caspian Sea, in Russia/Kazakhstan, 92 ft. below sea level
Main rivers: Elbe, Rhine, Danube, Volga
Largest country: Russia
Smallest country: Vatican State
Main languages: English, French, German, Russian
Industry: agriculture (wheat, barley, rye, livestock), manufacturing, fishing, mining coal and iron ore

Europe

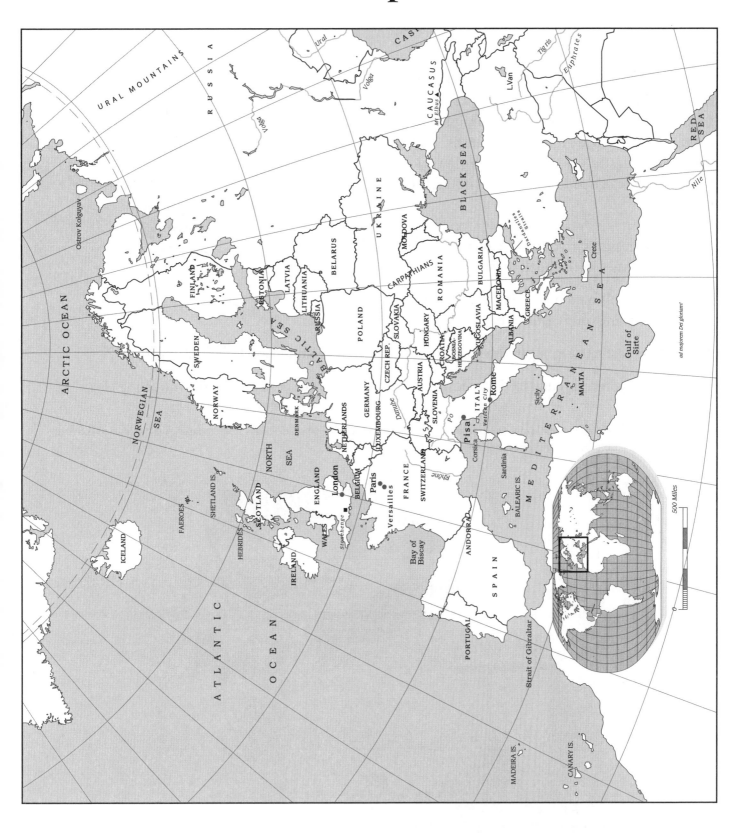

ARCTIC OCEAN

URAL MOUNTAINS

RUSSIA

Ural

Volga

CASPIAN

CAUCASUS
Mt Elbrus ▲

L. Van

Tigris

Euphrates

RED SEA

Nile

BLACK SEA

Ostrov Kolguyav

FINLAND

ESTONIA

LATVIA

LITHUANIA

RUSSIA

BELARUS

UKRAINE

MOLDOVA

CARPATHIANS

ROMANIA

BULGARIA

MACEDONIA

GREECE

Dardanelles Strait

Crete

SWEDEN

NORWAY

BALTIC SEA

POLAND

SLOVAKIA

HUNGARY

CZECH REP.

AUSTRIA

CROATIA

SLOVENIA

BOSNIA
HERZEGOVINA

YUGOSLAVIA

ALBANIA

M E D I T E R R A N E A N   S E A

Gulf of
Sirte

ad majorem Dei gloriam!

NORWEGIAN SEA

DENMARK

GERMANY

LUXEMBOURG

Danube

Rhône

Po

Rome
Vatican City

Pisa

ITALY

Sicily

Sardinia

Corsica

MALTA

NORTH SEA

SHETLAND IS.

SCOTLAND

ENGLAND

London

Stonehenge

NETHERLANDS

BELGIUM

Paris

Versailles

FRANCE

SWITZERLAND

BALEARIC IS.

FAEROES

HEBRIDES

WALES

IRELAND

Bay of
Biscay

ANDORRA

SPAIN

PORTUGAL

Strait of Gibraltar

ICELAND

ATLANTIC   OCEAN

MADEIRA IS.

CANARY IS.

500 Miles

©2012 Geography Matters®   GEOGRAPHY THROUGH ART   www.geomatters.com

EUROPE

Castles

There are many famous castles located on the continent of Europe. These are remnants of Europe's old feudal system. In the feudal system, when a king conquered a piece of land, he would divide it among his lords. Each lord would then build a castle. Castles differed from region to region, but all were designed to protect and house the noble family.

Materials
paper
pencil
cardboard or foam board
sugar cubes
white glue
modeling clay

1. Sketch a design for your castle on paper. Look at the famous castles in the book to give you some ideas.

2. Cut a piece of foam board or cardboard a little larger than you want your castle to be.

3. Build the castle using sugar cubes on the cardboard. Use white glue to hold it together.

4. If desired, you can sculpt lords, ladies, and livestock for your castle using the modeling clay.

Note: For a completely edible castle, use the edible glue recipe from the Gingerbread House in Germany. You can also make your figures using the edible clay recipe for Stonehenge in the England section.

Edinburgh Castle, Scotland

Blarney Castle, Ireland

Coat of Arms

You might want to design a Coat of Arms for your castle. A Coat of Arms was often used on shields, flags, and other items to identify the owner. Knights wore the Coat of the lord they fought for. Designs differed with each region and country. You can design a coat of arms for yourself or your family!

Materials
shield template
poster board or cardboard
scissors
pencil
markers

1. Trace the shield template onto a piece of poster board or cardboard.

2. Cut out the shield shape.

3. Use a pencil to sketch your design on the shield.
Shields were often divided into sections. This can be done in a number of ways. Divide the shield in half, quarters, thirds, or like pieces of a pie. It can be divided horizontally, vertically, or diagonally.

4. You might also wish to add a motto at the bottom of your shield. Many Coats of Arms bore a phrase or slogan that summed up the person's ideals or acted as a battle cry. These mottoes were usually written in Latin.

5. Use markers to color your design.

Colors & Symbols for a Coat of Arms

White: peace
Orange: worthiness
Yellow: generosity, wealth
Black: grief, suffering
Blue: truth
Green: hope
Red: military strength
Purple: royalty

Bear: protectiveness, loyalty
Bee: efficiency
Boar: tenacity
Dagger: justice
Deer: peace
Fox: cleverness
Lion: courage
Snake: wisdom

ENGLAND 🍴

Stonehenge ☆ ⓘ

Stonehenge, located near Salisbury England, is one of Britain's most famous structures. To this day, no one can say with certainty why or how these structures came to be. Is this an early form of architecture? Is it an ancient pagan temple? Is it an early, primitive clock or calendar? No one knows. We only know that it is a **megalithic structure**. A megalithic structure is made with huge stones that show little evidence of having been carved or sculpted. It appears they were simply brought in their natural state, set up in a design, and left without any mortar or other fastening agent. Sculpt your own version of Stonehenge with this edible clay.

Materials
foam board or cardboard
1 cup smooth peanut butter
1 1/3 cups powdered milk
3 tablespoons honey

1. Combine peanut butter, milk, and honey in a bowl. Mix thoroughly.

2. Sculpt your own version of Stonehenge on foam board or cardboard.

QUICKSKETCH: BIG BEN

This famous clock tower, located in London England, is commonly known as Big Ben. It is actually the name of one of the large bells of the clock's chimes. Big Ben is the world's largest chiming clock with four faces. Over the years, it has become a symbol of England, much like the Eiffel Tower has come to represent France. In your geography notebook, sketch Big Ben. Beside it, sketch a design for a clock tower of your own. Use your imagination.

Inn Sign ☆

When you think of artwork, the inn sign may not be the first thing that comes to mind. Even so, this everyday item can be a work of art. Inn signs in England have been around for many years. These signs often included pictures representing the name. This helped the many people who were unable to read. Animals were often used on the signs. For this project, make an inn sign for home.

Materials
poster board
pencils
markers
hole punch
string

1. Decide on a name and emblem for your sign. What animal most represents your family or home? What name is most appropriate?

2. Sketch your design on the poster board. Use big, bold letters for the name so it will be easy to read from the street.

3. Color the design with markers.

4. Punch a hole in each of the top corners of your sign. Tie a string through the holes for hanging.

5. Have an adult help you hang your sign. If you hang it outside the house, be sure to bring it in before it rains. You might also choose to hang it on your bedroom door.

☆☆☆ Older students may wish to make a real sign out of wood. They can carve their sign and paint it or use a wood-burning kit.

FRANCE 🍴

Palace at Versailles ☆☆

The Palace at Versailles may be the most famous palace in the world. It once belonged to Louis XIV. Build your own version of the Palace for this project.

1. Decide if you want to make an exact replica of the Palace at Versailles or if you want to make your own version. It might help to draw a sketch of want you want the finished palace to look like.

2. Gather up the empty boxes and cans. Put them together until they resemble a palace. Once you are happy with their look, glue them together.

3. When the glue has thoroughly dried, paint your palace.

4. Use a piece of foam board for the base of the castle, securing it with glue.

5. Landscape the foam board around your palace. Use paint, moss, rocks, sand, and twigs. Use your imagination. Look online or in a book to see what the gardens look like at the Palace at Versailles.

Materials
small empty boxes and cans (such as shoe boxes, coffee cans, cereal boxes)
foam board
moss, sand, rocks, twigs
glue
acrylic or poster paint
paintbrushes

The Art of Assemblage

The project for the Palace at Versailles is an example of **assemblage**. This is the art of making things from found objects (in this case, discarded containers). It is the three-dimensional relative to the collage, which we learned about in the projects for Butterfly Wing Art and Russian Mosaics.

QUICKSKETCH: EIFFEL TOWER

The Eiffel Tower is one of the most widely recognized landmarks in the world. It was built out of iron over a century ago for the Paris Exposition. At 100 stories high, it is the tallest structure in Paris. Draw a picture of the Eiffel Tower in your geography notebook. If you are feeling really creative, try to build the tower out of toothpicks. (You can use air-dry modeling clay to hold it together.)

Stained Glass Windows ☆

Stained glass windows are a beautiful form of art. These windows are usually found in cathedrals and portray religious themes. Amazing examples of stained glass are found in the cathedral at Chartres, France, which has 176 stained glass windows.

1. Draw a sketch on a regular piece of paper of what you want your stained glass to look like.

2. Using the sketch as a guide, color a piece of wax paper with your design. Press firmly to make the colors as dark as possible. Use black crayon to put dark lines in between each "glass" color.

3. When you are finished coloring the picture, place another piece of wax paper on top of it.

4. Have an adult iron the wax papers together. (Place a dish towel between the iron and the wax papers to keep the iron clean.)

5. After the papers have thoroughly cooled, cut your stained glass picture out from the waxed paper.

6. Make a frame out of construction paper by cutting a hole in the paper the size of your stained glass. Tape the stained glass to the back of the paper. You can hang the stained glass in the window with tape or string.

Materials

paper
pencil
wax paper
crayons
iron
scissors
construction paper
glue or tape

GERMANY 🍴

Gingerbread House ☆

Here is a great Christmas activity.

1. Rinse and dry the inside of the milk carton. (If it is a large carton, cut off the bottom to make it smaller.) Staple the top shut like it was before it was opened.

2. Make edible "glue" by beating the sugar, cream of tartar, egg white, and water on high speed for ten minutes.

3. Use the edible glue to fasten graham crackers to the carton.

4. Decorate the gingerbread house with candy, using the glue to secure the candy to the graham crackers.

Materials

small empty paper milk carton
(or cream carton)
stapler
1 cup powdered sugar
1/4 teaspoon cream of tartar
1 egg white
1/3 cup boiling water
graham crackers
pieces of candy
(peppermints, candy canes, gum drops, etc.)

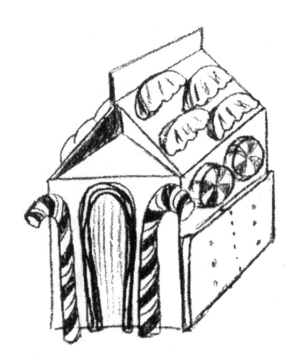

The Original Gingerbread House

Where did the idea for a gingerbread house come from? It probably originated from the famous fairy tale, Hansel and Gretel. The Brothers Grimm made this story, once a German folk tale, popular. In the story, a brother and sister, Hansel and Gretel, get lost in the forest. They stumble upon a house, not made of wood or brick, but of gingerbread. An evil witch built the house to lure the children in. Thankfully, the gingerbread houses we will make are much less dangerous.

GREECE

Fresco

A **fresco** is painting that is done in wet plaster. The word "fresco" actually comes from the Italian word for "fresh" because the painting is done in "fresh" plaster. Painting directly onto the wet plaster results in brighter colors. It also gives long life to a piece. Many frescoes in existence today are over a thousand years old! Fresco painting had to be done very quickly before the plaster dried. Thus, artists were not only talented, but speedy as well.

A Minoan Fresco ☆

Look on your map of Europe and find the island of Crete. It is located just below the country of Greece, in the Mediterranean Sea. The ancient Minoan civilization inhabited this Greek island, leaving behind beautiful artwork in the form of frescoes. Much of what we know about the culture of this civilization has been learned from these pieces of art.

Materials
**paper
pencils
plaster of Paris
styrofoam plates
acrylic paints
paintbrushes**

1. Choose a design for your painting. Sketch it on paper first so you will have an idea before you start working in the plaster.

2. Mix plaster of Paris according to the package directions. (You may also purchase it premixed.)

3. Pour the plaster into a styrofoam plate. Shake the plates gently from side to side to help get out any air bubbles.

4. Allow the plaster to harden slightly. Paint your design onto the plaster using acrylic paints. The paint will soak into the plaster.

5. Let dry thoroughly. Cut or pull away the plate. You now have your own Minoan fresco!

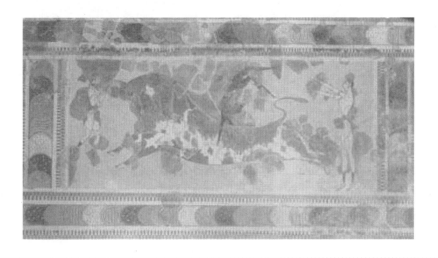

Parthenon ★☆ ⓘ

The Parthenon, in Athens Greece, is one of the most exceptional buildings in all of history. It is said to be proportionally perfect. It is representative of the incredible accomplishments of the ancient Greeks, both in architecture and other areas. It was built in honor of the Greek goddess Athena. In this project, you will learn to draw the Parthenon in two-point perspective. First you will draw a plain box, then you will fill it in with details of the Parthenon.

Horizon line: the line in a painting where the sky meets the ground
Orthogonal: the diagonal lines drawn from the vanishing point to the object
Two-point perspective: a drawing done with two vanishing points; looks very realistic
Vanishing point: the point on the horizon line at which visibility ends

1. Draw a horizon line on your paper. (fig. 1) Place a vanishing point at each end of the line. Mark each line lightly with pencil because we will be erasing them later. Place the front vertical corner of your box (a short straight line) on the page. If you place it below the horizon line, it will appear that we are looking down on the box. If you place it above the line, it will look like we are looking up at the box in the distance. If you place it on the line, as in the example, we will be looking straight ahead.

2. Draw an orthogonal, which is a diagonal line, from each vanishing point to the top and bottom of the short straight line. (fig. 2)

3. Place the ends of your box within the orthogonals. (fig. 3)

4. Erase the extra lines. You now have a box that you can fill in with details of the Parthenon. (fig. 4)

Culture Connection: NASHVILLE PARTHENON

Do you want to visit the Parthenon? If you don't have the resources to travel to Greece, you might try visiting Nashville, Tennessee. In Nashville is an exact replica of the Parthenon. The only difference is that the Nashville Parthenon is in better shape. It has not endured years of weather and other damaging things. It was built for the World's Fair of 1897 because of Nashville's nickname, "The Athens of the South."

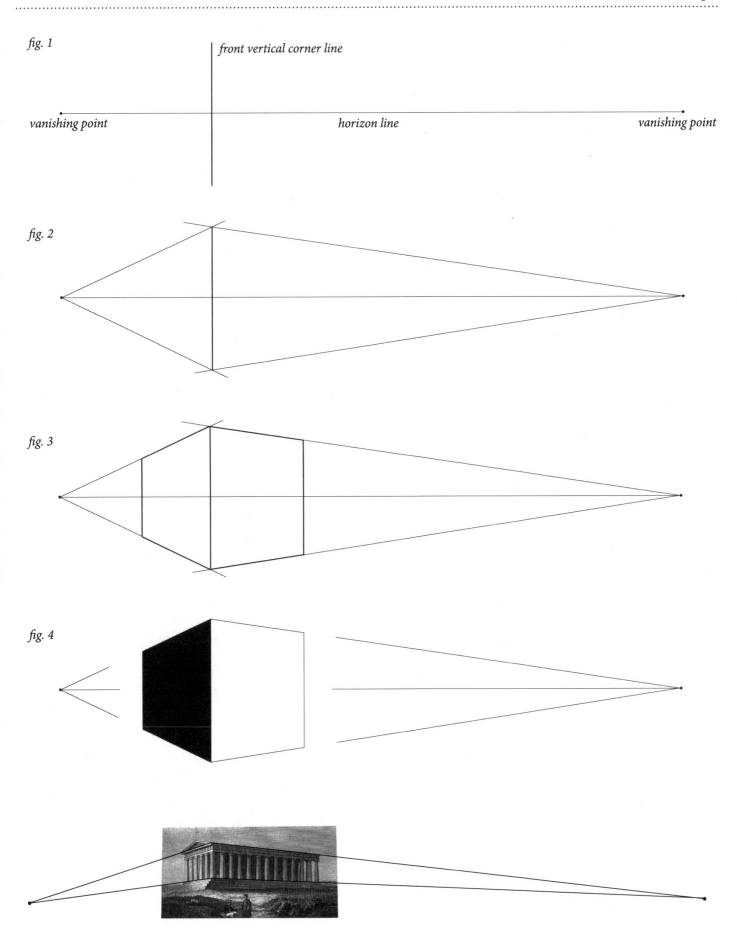

fig. 1

front vertical corner line

vanishing point   horizon line   *vanishing point*

fig. 2

fig. 3

fig. 4

ITALY 🍴

Sistine Chapel ☆

The Sistine Chapel is located in Italy at the home of the Pope, Vatican City. This beautiful chapel has many unique features, perhaps the most famous being the ceiling. Michelangelo, a well-known Italian artist, spent nearly four years from 1508-1512 painting the ceiling. It is decorated with nearly 300 figures from famous Bible stories.

Materials
**a large poster board or
piece of craft paper
poster paints
paintbrushes**

1. With your parent's permission, tape a poster board or large piece of craft paper to the bottom of the kitchen or dining room table. (A coffee table might work better for smaller students.)

2. Get paints and paintbrushes ready. Lie flat on your back underneath the table, and paint a picture of your favorite Bible story. (You can pick a story from another book if you choose.)

3. When you are finished, let the painting dry. Then carefully take it down and admire your finished work. (If your arms are tired, imagine that you are Michelangelo with only 299 paintings and 4 years left to work on this project!)

Note: To keep from getting paint on the floor, put a trash bag or old vinyl tablecloth underneath your work of art.

Artist Profile: MICHELANGELO

Michelangelo is an artist from the Italian Renaissance, a movement that revived an interest in learning and the arts after the Medieval Ages. While the Sistine Chapel may be the work with which we are most familiar, Michelangelo painted many other pieces and sculpted as well. In fact, he preferred sculpting to painting. He thought his own paintings inferior when compared to his sculptures.

Pieta

QUICKSKETCH: LEANING TOWER OF PISA

Construction began on the Leaning Tower in Pisa, Italy on August 9, 1173. It was built as a bell tower for a neighboring cathedral. The tower leans because it was built with a weak foundation on loose soil. Many attempts over the years have been made to straighten the tower, but all have failed. Some have actually caused the tower to lean more. It recent times, engineers have worked to strengthen the tower without straightening it. Many believe that to set the tower straight would be to ruin its historical value and the reason that most people visit it. Draw the Leaning Tower of Pisa in your geography notebook. To make the tower look more realistic, add shading like the tower on the right below.

Roman Concrete ☆☆

One of the great contributions of the Romans was in building materials. They used a strong material called caementicum. This type of concrete was made from volcanic ash, lime, water, and stones. Many structures made from this material have lasted until today. We see Roman domes, arches, and vaults that have stood on their own for centuries because of the strength of this material. Make your own version of a Roman brick with the recipe below. (This recipe comes from Robbie Blum in Denver, Colorado.)

Materials
1 cup flour
1/2 cup salt
1 cup used coffee grinds
1/2 cup cold, leftover coffee

1. Combine ingredients in a bowl and stir until well blended.

2. Knead the mixture by hand on a floured surface until smooth.

3. Shape into a brick.

4. Air dry or bake at 175 degrees for thirty minutes.

QuickSketch: Arch of Septimius Severus

The Romans loved to build arches. Triumphal arches were built for the Roman soldiers who had won important battles. The soldiers would march through them on their return to the city. The Arch of Titus was built to celebrate the conquest and destruction of Jerusalem. The Arch of Septimius Severus, shown on this page, was built to celebrate the military victories of the Emperor Severus and his sons. Draw this arch in your geography notebook.

Photo Archives of Famous Places of the World by Donald Witte

Roman Architecture

Roman architects used three types of columns to support their huge heavy buildings. They are are Doric, Ionic, and Corinthian. Doric columns are the most simple and the least attractive of the three. The Ionic columns generally have a scroll design and thinner longer shafts that sometimes have flutes, or vertical ridges. Corinthian columns are the most detailed and elaborate with fluted columns and ornate leaf designs. Over time column types have become mixed. You may find a Doric capitol on tall thin fluted shafts or an Ionic scroll and capitol on short, smooth shafts.

Mona Lisa Portrait ★★☆

What painting is reproduced and copied more than any other painting? What painting has made the most appearances in movies, television shows, and books? The *Mona Lisa*! This painting by Leonardo da Vinci is considered the most famous painting in the world. The mysterious smile of *Mona Lisa* is the subject of much controversy. What does her smile mean? We will probably never know, but we can try to mimic it in this art project. This painting is a great model to use for learning to draw a face. Make your pencil marks light so you can erase them later. Use figure two as a guide for these directions.

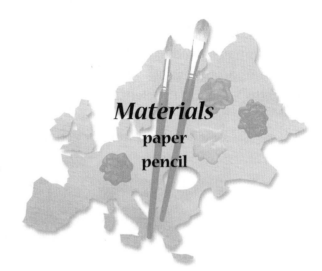

Materials
paper
pencil

1. Draw an oval for the face.

2. Divide the oval in half with a vertical line down the middle. This is where the nose goes. Divide the face in half horizontally—the eye line.

3. Make a line one-third up the face for the mouth. At the one-fourth mark, make a line for the nose.

4. Add the basic shape for the eyes first. Faces are usually five eyes wide. There is one eye space in between the two eyes, and an eye space on each side of the eyes. (In figure 3 notice that Mona's face is turned slightly to her right. This turning of the head makes it difficult to see that her head is five eyes wide.)

5. Add the nose. It will start at the eye line and extend down to the nose line.

6. Draw a line from the center of each eye down. In between these lines, at the mouth line, add the basic shape for a mouth.

7. Erase the lines from the face, leaving only the basic shapes of the features.

8. Fill in shapes with details. Add hair, eyelashes, eyebrows, and other details. Pay close attention to the details and shading on the *Mona Lisa* to help guide you.

Artist Profile: LEONARDO DA VINCI

Leonardo da Vinci may be the most famous painter in the history of the world. Like Michelangelo, he was a product of the Renaissance. In fact, he was considered the ultimate "Renaissance man"— a well-rounded person who excels at many different things. His interests were by no means limited to art, but included science, history, nature, anatomy, and inventing. He left behind thousands of pages of his notes and observations on a wide range of topics, complete with sketches. His most famous paintings are the *Mona Lisa* and *The Last Supper*.

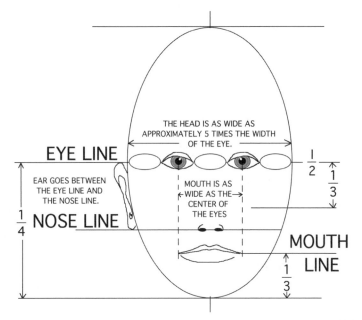

THE HEAD IS AS WIDE AS APPROXIMATELY 5 TIMES THE WIDTH OF THE EYE.

EYE LINE

EAR GOES BETWEEN THE EYE LINE AND THE NOSE LINE.

NOSE LINE

MOUTH IS AS WIDE AS THE CENTER OF THE EYES

$\frac{1}{2}$ $\frac{1}{3}$

$\frac{1}{4}$

MOUTH LINE

$\frac{1}{3}$

fig. 1

fig. 3

eye line 1/2
nose line 1/4

mouth line bottom 1/3

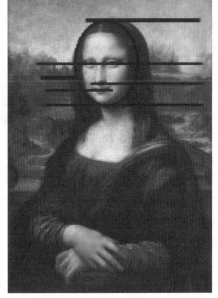

fig. 2

POLAND

Polish Paper Cutting ☆☆ ⓘ

Wycinanki is the Polish folk art of paper cutting. The poorer classes of people started making paper cut designs to decorate their homes because they could not afford traditional art. Birds, trees, chickens, and flowers are all common in these Polish paper cuts. There are two types of paper cuts. One is made from one solid color paper. The other is made from many different colors layered on top of each other. For this project, we will make a design in one color.

Materials
tracing paper
pencil
scissors
glue
construction paper
colored pencils

1. If desired, you can download a template by visiting our WebLinks page. If not, draw your own by looking at an example on this page. Trace the design onto tracing paper, leaving off the small details that would be difficult to cut. You may want to enlarge the example before tracing it.

2. Cut the design from the tracing paper. Glue to a piece of colored construction paper.

3. Decorate the paper cutting with colored pencils.

SWEDEN

Viking Ivory Chessmen ☆☆

On this page is an example of chessmen made by the Vikings. Since the Vikings were a great seafaring people, they probably brought the game of chess back with them on one of their voyages. (The game originated in Northern Indian or Afghanistan about 600 AD.)

Materials
paper
pencil
modeling clay

1. On a sheet of paper, draw a design for your chess piece. Use the Viking examples on this page for inspiration.

2. Make your chess piece out of modeling clay. Use toothpicks to carve out small details.

3. Cure according to the clay directions.

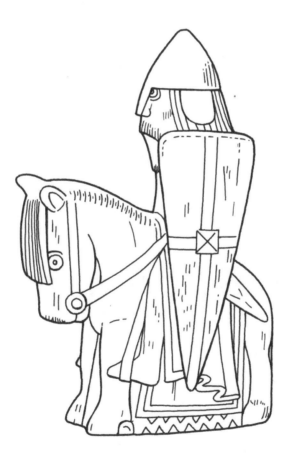

Viking Rune Stones ☆☆ ⓘ

Runes are the letters of the Viking alphabet. You might notice from the illustrations that some of the letters are very similar to the letters of the English alphabet. This is because both alphabets were based on Greek and Latin roots. Runes were often carved onto everyday objects. Notice the lack of curves in the runes. Only straight lines were used to make them easy to carve. Rocks were one of the more common things that were carved.

1. Form the clay into the shape of a rock. A thin, oval shape would probably be best.

2. Using toothpicks, etch some runes into your rock.

3. Let your "rock" dry thoroughly. (If it is the kind of clay that you bake, bake according to the directions and then allow to cool.)

4. When the clay has hardened, use black paint and a small paintbrush to paint etchings. This will help them stand out from the rock.

Materials
modeling clay-
(gray or any rocklike color)
toothpicks
black paint
small paintbrush

a b c d e f g h ij k l m

n o p q r s t uvw x y z

The Vikings

In world history, the Vikings are considered violent marauders and warriors. They originated from the area around Sweden. The Viking Age was from the ninth to eleven century. During that time, the Vikings invaded and colonized a large portion of Europe. The Viking people were great seamen, as well as tradesmen and craftsmen. The carved rune stones were just one example of their craftsmanship.

Culture Connection: RUNE STONE

What do the rune stones remind you of? What about the Egyptian carved orthostats? Giant rune stones were often used to mark graves, much like the orthostats were used to label tombs.

Runes were also used as a primitive form of something you might find surprising—graffiti! As the Vikings invaded new territories, they would often deface whatever stood in their path with runes—rocks, trees, buildings, etc. In fact, many statues throughout Europe are covered in runes. Rune graffiti was even left in cathedrals.

SWITZERLAND

Painting

Look at the beautiful design on this page from the Alpine region of Switzerland. Notice the **symmetry**. Symmetry is when something is identical on both sides. In this project, you will make your own symmetric designs.

Materials
paper
pencil
small paintbrush
paint

1. Fold the paper in half.

2. On one half of the paper, draw half of your design. (For example, draw half of a flower.) Draw all the way up to the folded edge.

3. Now paint along the lines you have drawn.

4. While the paint is still wet, press the painted side onto the unpainted side. You now have a symmetrical flower design. Fill in the lines with color if desired.

UKRAINE

Easter Eggs ☆

Easter Eggs are a popular tradition in the Ukraine. Ukrainian people have exchanged Easter Eggs, called pysanky, for hundreds of years. Eggs were given to the local priests, neighbors, and family and were even placed on the graves of deceased loved ones.

1. Cut out the shape of an egg. (Make more than one for extra fun.)

2. Decorate and paint the egg. Use the colors and symbols listed below to give you some ideas.

3. When you have finished decorating your egg, punch a hole in the top and tie a loop with gold ribbon.

Materials
white cardstock
watercolor paints
paintbrushes
hole punch
gold ribbon

Colors:

White: purity   Blue: health
Orange: strength   Green: hope
Yellow: light   Red: happiness
Black: eternity

Symbols:

Ladder: prayer   Butterfly: Poppy flowers:
Cross: Jesus   resurrection of   joy
Christ   Christ   Sunflowers: life
Triangle: the   Horse or Deer: Diamonds:
Holy Trinity   wealth   knowledge
Fish: Jesus Christ Grapes: goodwill   Hearts: love

     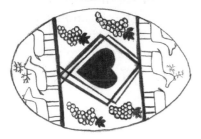

Culture Connection: INDIAN BATIK

Ukrainian eggs are usually decorated using a wax-resist method, similar to Indian batik. Hot beeswax was applied to the eggs in a pattern. The eggs were then dyed and the wax was removed, leaving a design where the wax had been. This process was repeated several times until the desired effect was achieved.

Artist Profile: PETER CARL FABERGE

Peter Carl Faberge is perhaps the most famous decorator of eggs in the world. He made eggs for the wealthiest families in Russia, mainly the royal families. He and his assistants created a total of sixty-eight eggs between 1885 and 1917. A jeweler by trade, Faberge's eggs were often coated with precious metals and then decorated with gemstones. These intricate eggs usually opened up to reveal an equally delicate surprise. Add a little Faberge pizzazz to your egg by gluing on glitter and sequins. ℹ

NORTH AMERICA

Continent Summary

The 9.5 million miles that make up North America include Greenland, Canada, USA, Mexico, and Central America. The islands of the Caribbean Sea, known for their diverse culture of Africans, Europeans, and Indians are considered part of Central America. Bounded by the Pacific Ocean to the West and the Atlantic Ocean on the East, this 3rd largest continent is connected to South America by a narrow isthmus at its southernmost point.

The physical features of North America vary. Major rivers include the Yukon in Canada and Alaska; Mackenzie and Saskatchewan in Canada; St. Lawrence and Columbia in Canada and U.S.; and Rio Grande at the U.S./Mexican border. Can you locate these on your map? The Mississippi, weaving north to south through the United States, is the continent's longest river. Major mountains include Appalachians in the east (Newfoundland through Georgia); Rockies stretching from western Canada into Mexico; and Sierra Madres spanning Mexico into Central America like a spiny volcanic backbone. The highest point is Mt. McKinley, Alaska (20,320 ft.) and the lowest point is in Death Valley, California (282 ft. below sea level). Why do you suppose it is called Death Valley?

North America is the most wealthy and influential continent of the world because of its temperate climate, abundance of natural resources, technological innovations, and energy supplies. Manufacturing includes chemical industries, military equipment, automobiles, and books to name a few. The Great Plains are known as the "Breadbasket of the World" for its vast farmland. The U.S. and Canada export tons of surplus grain, beans, sugar, and fruit. Central America is a region of volcanic rugged mountains, which contribute to a variable tropical climate. Low-lying areas may have tropical rainforest vegetation while drier areas of Yucatan region of Mexico have shrub vegetation. The people of this region must deal with hurricanes almost yearly. Central America's mostly agricultural economy depends upon the U.S. to buy its exports.

North America has some interesting world records. Greenland, the largest island in the world at 840,000 square miles, is over two and a half times the size of the next largest island. The world's greatest rise in temperature and greatest drop in temperature ever recorded in a 12-hour period occurred in North America. In 1918 Granville, North Dakota's temperatures was 33° below zero in the morning and soared to 83° by late afternoon! In Fairfield, Montana, on Christmas Eve in 1924 the temperature dropped from 63° at noon to 2° below zero by midnight. Do you know how many degrees difference that is? (65)

Central America boasts of one of the world's greatest engineering achievements. It is the Panama Canal. The 40-mile canal, which significantly shortened the 12,000-mile journey around the tip of South America, opened to ship traffic in 1914. More than 30 oceangoing vessels take this shortcut between the Atlantic and Pacific oceans each day. Fifty-two million gallons of fresh water are moved to raise each ship 85 feet above sea level to cross the canal. Log on to www.landmarkcams.com/category/panama-canal-cams to learn more about this engineering masterpiece and see live images of ship traffic move through the canal.

Facts
Size: 9,500,000 square miles
Rank: 3rd largest continent
Highest point: Mount McKinley, Alaska 20,320 ft.
Longest cave system: under Mammoth Cave National Park in Kentucky, 348 miles
Longest river: Mississippi 2348 miles
Main rivers: Mississippi, Ohio, Missouri
Largest country: Canada
Smallest country: St. Kitts and Nevis
Main languages: Creole, English, French, Spanish
Industry: computing, technology, chemical industries, metal fabrication, agriculture

North America

ARCTIC OCEAN

Ellesmere Island

GREENLAND

ALASKA

Yukon

Mt. McKinley
20,320 ft.

Mackenzie

Yukon

C A N A D A

Saskatchewan

ROCKY

Seattle

Columbia

Missouri

Granville

MONTANA

Fairfield

N. DAKODA

S. DAKODA

Rapid City

CASCADE RANGE

M
O
U
N
T
A
I
N
S

Missouri

Mississippi

St. Lawrence

Niagra Falls

PENNSYLVANIA

New York City

Philadelphia

Washington DC

SIERRA NEVADA

PACIFIC OCEAN

Mt. Whitney

Death Valley

Colorado

Great Plains

St. Louis

Ohio

Mammoth
Cave

UNITED STATES OF
AMERICA

APPA

ATLANTIC OCEAN

Tropic of Cancer

Mississippi

Rio Grande

SIERRA

MEXICO

GULF OF MEXICO

CUBA

ST. KITTS
AND NEVIS

MADRE

CARIBBEAN SEA

Lake
Atitlan

Central America

GUATEMALA

Panama Canal

0   500   1000 Miles

ad majorem Dei gloriam!

PANAMA

GEOGRAPHY THROUGH ART

CANADA

Maple Leaf Rubbings ☆

The Canadian flag features a maple leaf in the center. Thus, the maple leaf has become a symbol that represents Canada all over the world. For this project, you will do a maple leaf rubbing.

1. Lay your leaves on the table. Arrange them in the design that you want.

2. Place a piece of paper on top of the leaves.

3. Rub crayons over the leaves until you see the design of the leaf. Do each leaf the same color, or use different colors for variety.

Materials
maple leaves in various sizes
crayons
paper

Note: If there isn't a maple leaf available to you, trace and color one of the maple leaves on this page. Overlap several maple leaf tracings to make a pattern.

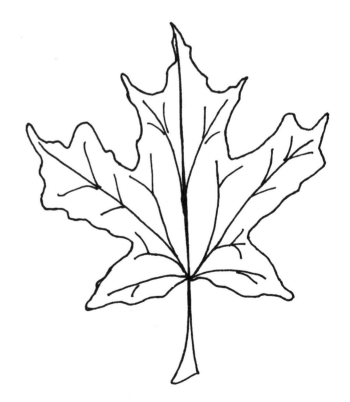

QUICKSKETCH: MOOSE

Moose can be found in most of Canada and in some parts of the northern United States. The moose is the largest member of the deer family. It has a unique antler shape. Draw a moose in your geography notebook.

GUATEMALA 🍴

Huipil Weaving ☆

The huipil (Wee-peel) is a piece of cloth woven in Guatemala. It is usually woven by hand. These beautiful garments are often embroidered with images from nature and everyday life. Bright colors are always used. The designs on a huipil are very personal. You can tell from the designs what family a person is from, what village they live in, and what religion they practice.

1. With pencil and paper, design a huipil for yourself. Be sure to include things that are personal to you.

2. Color your huipil with markers.

Materials
paper
pencil
markers

Lake Atitlan

Lake Atitlan is a beautiful lake located in the country of Guatemala. It is the deepest lake in Central America. It is estimated to be as deep as 1,100 feet in some places. The lake has several volcanoes surrounding it.

MEXICO 🍴

Wall Hanging ☆

On this page is a lovely example of a Mexican wall hanging. These pieces, often pictures of villages, are painted on burlap. In this wall hanging, the church is in the center with all the homes, people, and animals around it.

1. Sketch your design on a scrap piece of paper. You can do a picture of your neighborhood, church, or other group. Place the central object in the middle. Around it, place the individual homes and buildings. Be sure to include the people that are important to you.

2. Trim the burlap to the size that you want. (Zigzag the edges with pinking shears if desired.)

3. Paint your picture onto the wall hanging. Be sure to use bright colors.

4. Hang the picture by framing it or placing string through holes in the top.

Materials
pencil
paper
1/2 yard burlap
scissors or pinking shears
acrylic paint
paintbrushes

Oaxacan Woodcarvings ☆

A wonderful Mexican folk art is the Oaxacan woodcarving, named for the region of the country it comes from. These delightful creatures are carved from Copal tree wood. Each creature is usually a basic, primitive shape. The designs on the bodies are what really make them interesting. Each creature is covered with different patterns, whether it is dots, stripes, checks, etc. The creatures are painted with bright, vivid colors.

Materials
paper
pencil
markers

1. Draw the basic outline of an animal.

2. Fill in the outline with a pattern.

3. Color your animal with bright colors.

☆☆☆ For a more challenging project, have students make their creature out of modeling clay.

Papel Picado ☆

How do people in Mexico celebrate a special occasion? One way is with a Papel Picado banner. Papel Picado literally means "pierced paper." It is a piece of paper that has been cut with a pattern. Mexican families take many Papel Picados, put them on a string, and use them as a banner. This is a fun and affordable way to decorate for a party or holiday!

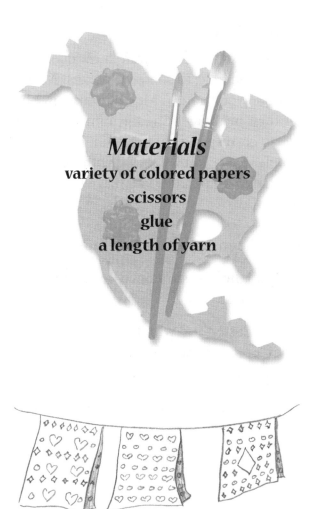

Materials
variety of colored papers
scissors
glue
a length of yarn

1. You can use any size paper, but it is best to start with a manageable size, such as standard 8 1/2" by 11". Fold it end-to-end as shown in the diagram on this page.

2. Cut a design of your choice only on the folded edge of the paper.

3. Unfold your paper. You may choose to cut a design around the edges. (Pinking shears or other shaped scissors are great for this.)

4. Cut a length of yarn as long as you want your banner to be.

5. Glue your Papel Picados to the yarn at the top of each piece. Let dry thoroughly and hang your banner!

Note: Authentic Papel Picados are done on tissue paper. This is a great use for leftover holiday tissue paper. Younger students, however, will probably find it too delicate to cut and fold, so printer or construction paper (or even leftover wrapping paper) should be used.

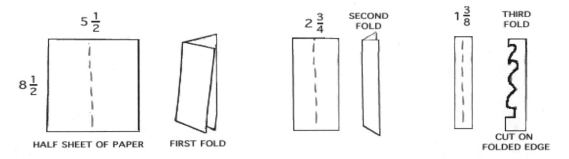

$5\frac{1}{2}$

$8\frac{1}{2}$

HALF SHEET OF PAPER   FIRST FOLD

$2\frac{3}{4}$ SECOND FOLD

$1\frac{3}{8}$ THIRD FOLD

CUT ON FOLDED EDGE

Culture Connection: CUT PAPER

Are you surprised to see another project involving cut paper? We have studied different forms of paper cutting from several countries—China, Poland, and now Mexico. We also discussed briefly the cut paper snowflakes frequently made by children in the United States. Why do you think paper cutting is such a popular art form? What is it about paper cutting that transcends cultures? Do you think it is the affordability and availability of paper? Could it be that cutting paper is easier than other forms of art? Or is it the fact that it can be done more quickly than something like a painting or sketch? Think of some other reasons why paper cutting is so common.

God's Eye ☆

God's Eye is a popular craft in Mexico. It is said that to give a God's Eye to someone means "May the eye of God be upon your home." Mexican's also give one to children for their birthday using the number of colors in the God's Eye to correspond with the child's age. To learn this simple weave you will begin with just two sticks. When you have had practice you may weave up to five sticks at a time.

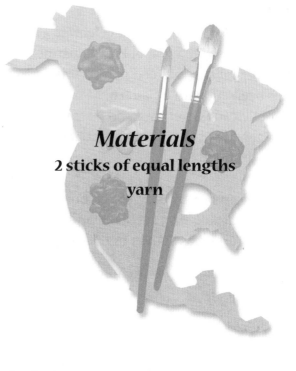

Materials
2 sticks of equal lengths
yarn

1. Tie the sticks together in a cross shape.

2. Wrap the first stick once, going over rather than under the stick.

3. Repeat step two with the remaining sticks. Keep wrapping the sticks until you have formed a diamond shape with the yarn and covered all the sticks.

4. Tie the yarn onto the last stick, cut off and tuck excess into the design.

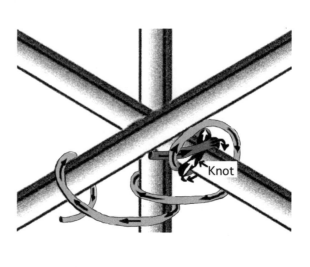

Knot

PANAMA

Mola ☆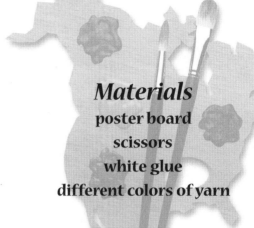

What is a mola? It is a woman's blouse from the country of Panama. Women from the Kuna region make these special blouses. They use appliqué and different fabrics to make these beautiful designs. They use the brightest colors they can find! Look at the designs on this page. Notice how everything is made with lines and patterns. Keep this in mind as you are working on your project.

1. Cut poster board to the size you want.

2. Draw your design on the poster board. You can use the designs on this page as templates if you want.

3. Trace the lines with a thin line of glue. Place pieces of yarn along the lines. Be sure to use different brightly colored yarns. Let dry.

Materials
poster board
scissors
white glue
different colors of yarn

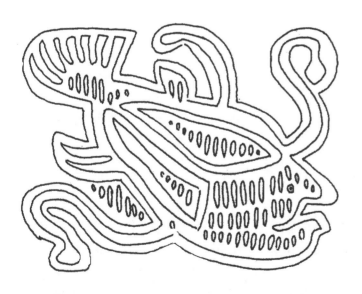

QUICKSKETCH: SLOTH

The sloth is a unique animal found in Central and South America. The name is very fitting, because sloths really are slothful. These creatures, which live in trees, sleep for up to eighteen hours a day. Even when they are awake, they move very little. They eat leaves and insects from the trees. Draw a sloth in your geography notebook.

UNITED STATES 🍴

Native American Sand Painting ☆

Native American tribes in the Southwestern United States usually practice sand painting. The art was once done as a part of important religious and cultural ceremonies. Now, it is an important source of income for the tribes, who sell the completed works to tourists. Be sure to use some of the signs and symbols you learned in the previous lesson in your sand painting project. This is a great project to do outdoors so you don't have to worry about making a mess with the sand.

Materials
foam board
pencil
colored sand
white glue
paintbrushes

1. Have an adult cut a piece of foam board to the size that you want for your sand painting.

2. Lightly draw your design on the foam board with a pencil.

3. Pick out the first color of sand you want to use. It is best to start with whatever color you will use the most. Place glue on each part of the painting you want to be that color. Sprinkle the one color of sand on the painted areas. Let dry.

4. Repeat step 3 using the next color of sand. Continue until your entire foam board is covered.

Note: Colored craft sand can be purchased inexpensively in the crafts section of most craft stores.

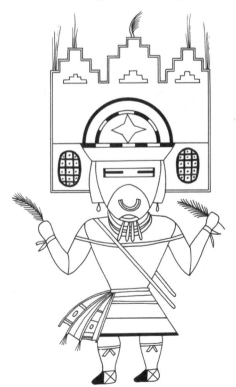

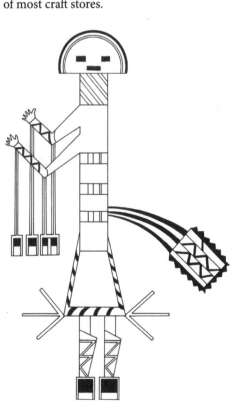

Native American Hide Paintings ☆

Native Americans wore buffalo hides to keep them warm. The hides were more than functional; they were also beautiful pieces of art. Hides were often painted with designs and symbols. A warrior's hide, for example, might contain illustrations of his greatest victories.

A tribal chief's hide would tell the history of the tribe. Often one single symbol would be painted on these hides to represent the most important event of the year. The next year, a new symbol would be painted beside it. Often a person's birth year was remembered as one of these symbols. A person might be able to point to the flooding symbol and say, "I was born the year of the great flood."

Materials
brown craft paper
pencil
charcoal pencil

1. Tear a piece of brown craft paper (or an old paper grocery bag) in the shape of an animal hide.

2. Soak the paper in sudsy water for half an hour. Wad it into a ball and let dry.

3. Using the symbols on the next page, draw a design on the paper in pencil.

4. When you are satisfied with your design, go over it with a black charcoal pencil.

Thunderbird
Sacred bearer of
unlimited happiness

Bird
Carefree,
lighthearted

Deer Track
Plentiful game

Bear Track
Good omen

Crossed Arrows
Friendship

Arrow
Protection

Cactus
Sign of the desert

Snake
Defiance, wisdom

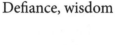

Thunderbird Track
Bright prospects

Rattlesnake Jaw
Strength

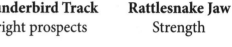

Eagel Feathers
Chief

Rain
Plentiful crops

Horse
Journey

Days & Nights
Time

Big Mountain
Abundance

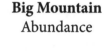

**Lightening &
Lightening Arrow**
Swiftness

Rain Clouds
Good prospects

Medicine Man's Eye
Wise, watchful

Man
Human life

Butterfly
Everlasting life

Culture Connection: HMONG STORY CLOTH

What is another thing we have studied that tells a story and can be worn? What about the Hmong story cloth? These are similar to the Native American hide paintings. Many archeologists believe that North America was once connected to Asia by land. Is it possible, then, that these two groups were once one? Is this the same kind of art done on different materials because of what was readily available?

Scrimshaw ★☆☆

Scrimshaw, from the Alaska region, is the art of carving ivory. Sailors originally started using scrimshaw during their long ocean voyages. They would carve images into whatever piece of ivory they could find—often whale teeth. Not surprisingly, the images were often nautical in nature. Whales, ship, and seascapes were all common.

1. Sketch the design you want to do on paper. Try to choose something with an ocean theme.

2. Shape the clay. You can do the shape of a large whale's tooth or even a bone. You could also shape it into a piano key. (Because ivory is so expensive and in some cases illegal, scrimshawing is often done on old ivory piano keys.)

3. Using a very sharp pencil, or a toothpick, etch your design into the clay.

4. Dry the clay according to the directions of the manufacturer.

5. When the clay is thoroughly dried, paint the etchings black.

Materials
paper
pencil
white or cream modeling clay
black acrylic paint
a small paintbrush

Eskimo Plate ★☆

The image below is taken from a carved Eskimo plate made of argillite, a soft slate. Notice the carved design of a killer whale. It was common for Eskimos to use whales and fish in their carvings. Design your own Eskimo plate.

1. Sketch the design you want to do on paper. Use an animal that is common in your area.

2. Make the clay. Form into the shape of a plate.

3. Using a very sharp pencil, or a toothpick, carve your design into the clay.

4. Dry the clay according to the directions in the recipe.

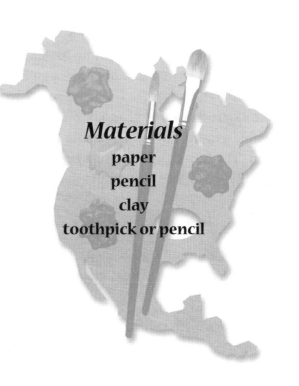

Materials
paper
pencil
clay
toothpick or pencil

Pennsylvania Dutch Hex Signs ☆

The Pennsylvania Dutch came to America from the country of Germany many years ago and settled in and around Pennsylvania. There are many wonderful examples of folk art from this group of people. Perhaps the most visible example of Pennsylvania Dutch folk art is the hex sign. The hex sign, so named because the designs are usually six-sided, is often painted on a barn to decorate it.

1. Cut a circle out of cardboard or foam board.

2. Draw a design on the circle in pencil. Use the examples below and on the next page for ideas.

3. Paint your design. The most common colors used in hex signs are red, yellow, blue, and green.

Materials
cardboard or foam board
scissors
pencils
acrylic or poster paints

Hex Signs Colors & Symbols

Colors:

Red: love

Green: growth

Yellow: health

Blue: peace, heaven

Brown: harvest, nature

White: purity

Violet: faith

Symbols:

Stars: good fortune

Tulips: faith

Birds: good luck

Hearts: love

Water drops: crop abundance

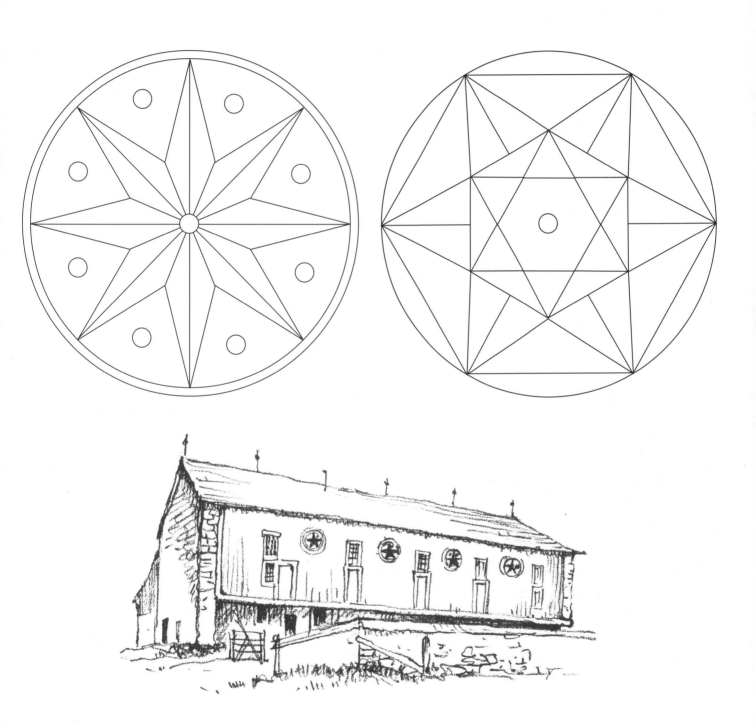

Pennsylvania Dutch Fraktur ★★

Fraktur is another beautiful type of folk art from the Pennsylvania Dutch people, dating form the 1700s. It is the decoration and illustration of important texts—usually birth, marriage, and baptism certificates. Religious ministers often decorated these records. Schoolteachers also practiced the art of fraktur, as rewards for good students, or to help teach different subjects.

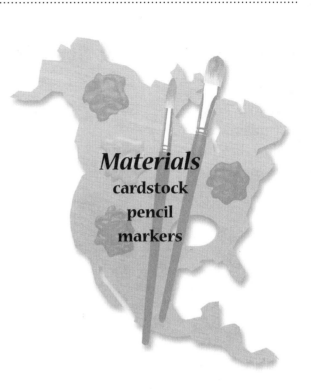

Materials
cardstock
pencil
markers

1. Decide what subject you want to use for your fraktur. Look online or in a library book for more examples to inspire you. A good choice might be a birth certificate.

2. Use pencil to design the fraktur. (Make light marks that can be erased later.) Write the text first. Here is a sample text for a birth certificate:

> (Your name here) was born on
> (birth date) at (time of birth)
> to
> (the name of your parents).
> (city of birth)

3. You might include a Scripture or quote on it as well.

4. Add decorations to the fraktur.

5. Color in the pencil marks with markers. Erase any visible pencil marks when you are finished. You might want to give a completed fraktur as a gift to new parents or a recently married couple.

Note: Some students might get frustrated making their letters look "fancy." To make this assignment easier, especially for younger students, print out a "birth certificate" on the cardstock in advance. Use a fancy calligraphy script. Have the students decorate the pre-printed certificate.

Culture Connection: ILLUMINATION

The art of fraktur is linked to a much older art which dates to the Medieval Age. It is the art of illumination. An illuminated text was often embellished with designs and calligraphic letters. This special art, often done in monasteries, was expensive and usually only reserved for very important books, such as prayer books or the Bible. It is thought that old illuminated texts might have been the inspiration for the more modern art of fraktur.

Jane Doe was born on
July 4, 1776 at 4 pm
to
Joe & Jamie Doe
Philadelphia, PA

Patchwork Quilt ☆

Quilting is a wonderful part of American heritage. Originally, quilts were not really considered pieces of art—they were simply meant to keep you warm. Quilts were affordable because they were often made from scrap pieces of fabric. A favorite quilt might contain pieces of baby clothes, work shirts, flour sacks, maybe even a wedding dress. Over time, quilting has developed into a true art form. There is a huge variety in patterns, fabric choices, and embellishments. The only thing that limits a quilt's design is your imagination!

Materials
graph paper
pencil
construction paper
scissors
glue
markers

1. Using graph paper, draw a design for a quilt square. (You can use your own graph paper or make a copy of the graph paper in the Appendix.) Remember to make big, bold shapes so that they will be easy to cut.

2. Cut a piece of construction paper into a square. Use a neutral color that will make a good backdrop for your design. On it, draw the design from your scrap paper.

3. Cut pieces of construction paper to fit on your design. Use different colors for added interest.

4. Glue the quilt "pieces" that you cut out onto your design. Be sure to cover up or erase all pencil markings. Make marks like thread would leave (- - - -) along the edges of the pieces using markers. This will help it look like you really sewed the square together.

5. If desired, make more paper "quilt squares" and put them together on a piece of poster board to make a wall hanging.

☆☆☆ Older students can use their design to make a real quilt square out of fabric.

Cornhusk Doll ☆☆

Cornhusk dolls were originally made by the Native Americans many years ago. When the Pilgrims came to North America, they also learned how to make the dolls. Cornhusk dolls were popular toys because they were easy to make and there was usually plenty of corn available. For this project, you will need dried corn husks. You may be able to purchase these at a grocery or craft store, or you can dry your own. Separate the silks (the stringy parts) from the husks and lay them in the sun to dry for a few days. You can use strips of brown paper bag or construction paper instead of corn husks. If you are using dried corn husks, soak them in warm water until soft, about ten minutes.

Materials
dried corn husks (10-12 per doll)
water
scissors
string or heavy thread
markers

1. Place four husks together with pointed ends down. Tie together near the top with string. Trim the top edges.

2. Flip the doll so that the tied end is facing down. Now fold the pointed ends down over the string. When all four husks have been folded down, tie another string close to the top to form a head. (You can stuff the head with small bits of husk or even a cotton ball to help get the desired shape.)

3. For the arms, cut a husk into three thin strips. Braid the strips, tying at both ends. Slide this in between the husks directly below the head. Bunch the doll and tie again below the arms.

4. Tie four more husks, pointed ends facing down, to the doll's waist to form a skirt.

5. If desired, tie on small bits of corn husk to hide your strings. Leave plain, or decorate by adding a face with markers. You can also make clothes for your cornhusk doll out of fabric.

5

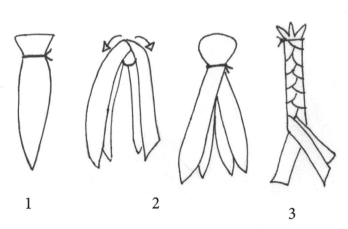

1   2

3

4

Easy Log Cabin ☆

The log cabin is thought to have originated in the Pennsylvania region. It is a house built from logs. In early America, it was a popular dwelling because it was easy to build and practical. Even today, log cabins are popular types of homes.

1. Cut some brown construction paper into strips. These will be your logs.

2. On a sky blue piece of construction paper, make a log cabin. Use paper strips and glue.

3. Cut out green paper for the grass to put under the log cabin.

4. Color in extra details with colored pencils.

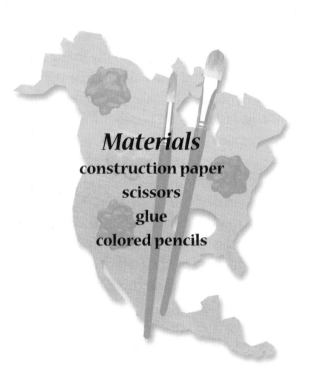

Materials
construction paper
scissors
glue
colored pencils

A Model Log Cabin ☆☆

If you enjoyed designing a log cabin on paper, you might try building a real model.

1. Cut a piece of foam board or cardboard to hold your cabin.

2. Build a real three-dimensional log cabin on the foam board or cardboard. Use sticks, wood scraps, and glue. A very tasty alternative is to build the log cabin with pretzel sticks. Use peanut butter for glue.

3. Landscape around the cabin with moss and rocks. You can even make paper or clay animals to put in the yard.

Materials
foam board or heavy cardboard
pencil
glue
construction materials
(**wood, twigs, moss, rocks**)

QuickSketch: Antebellum Architecture

Antebellum is a Latin term meaning, "before war." In the case of the United States, it refers to the time period before the Civil War. Architecture in this style generally refers to the old Southern plantation homes. These majestic and stately homes capture the slow, gracious lifestyle of the South. In your geography notebook, draw an antebellum home like one on this page.

Chainsaw Carving ☆☆☆

Chainsaw carving is a delightful form of American Ozark folk art. Chainsaw carving is just what the name implies—woodcarvings done with chainsaws. The nature of the work creates simple, primitive shapes. Nature is a common theme, especially bears, wolves, and fish.

Materials
large bar of soap
butter knife

1. Decide on a design for your carving. You might want to sketch it on scrap paper first.

2. Carve the design out of the bar of soap. (Do not use a sharp knife that could cut you!)

3. Your design should use the entire bar of soap. When it is finished, it should look more like a small sculpture than a picture just etched in the front of the soap.

Note: Chainsaws are a potentially dangerous piece of machinery. Students should never attempt to do a real chainsaw carving. Only trained adult professionals with proper safety gear should use a chainsaw for carving.

Ozarks

The Ozarks are located in the central highlands of the U.S. This geographic region covers the southern half of Missouri, the northern part of Arkansas and a small portion of Kansas and Oklahoma. It is also known as Ozark Mountains, or Ozark Mountain Country.

QUICKSKETCH: MOUNT RUSHMORE

Mount Rushmore is a solid granite cliff 25 miles west of Rapid City, South Dakota. Carved into the cliff are the faces of four U.S. Presidents—George Washington, Thomas Jefferson, Abraham Lincoln, and Theodore Roosevelt. George Washington's head is nearly sixty feet tall! Gutzon Borglum began this memorial in 1927 and worked on it for 14 years until he died in 1941. His son, Lincoln Borglum, completed his work. Draw a picture of Mount Rushmore in your geography notebook.

If you were going to make another Mount Rushmore, what famous people would you include? Draw a picture of your own Mount Rushmore.

QUICKSKETCH: WASHINGTON MONUMENT

The Washington Monument was built in honor of the first U.S. president, George Washington. It is located in Washington, D.C. The structure, 555 feet tall, is made from sandstone, granite, and marble. Architect Robert Mills designed it. Construction on the monument took over thirty years. It was completed in 1885. The long construction time was partly due to a lack of funds caused by the Civil War. When it was completed, it was the tallest structure in the world. The Eiffel Tower, however, soon took away the title. Draw a picture of the Washington Monument in your geography notebook.

If you were going to build a monument for a president or other leader, whom would you choose? What would the monument look like? Draw it in your geography notebook.

Central Park ☆

When you think of art, a park may not be the first thing that comes to mind. Some parks, however, are designed and laid out much like an artist would design a painting or sculpture. Central Park, located in New York City, is one such park. More visitors come to the park every year than any other park in the United States. The park, designed by Frederick Law Olmstead, is a place for busy New Yorkers to relax in a natural setting. The park has many features including a zoo, ice skating rinks, ponds, playgrounds, and amphitheaters. There are sports fields, tennis courts, and walking paths. The park is decorated with all kinds of plants, trees, and statues. For this project, design a park of your own.

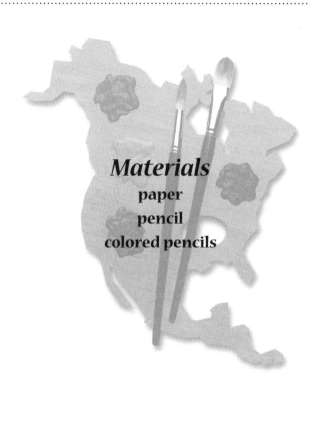

Materials
paper
pencil
colored pencils

1. Use a pencil to design a park on paper. Use a bird's-eye view, like you are looking down at the park from the sky. Be sure to label each part of your park. Don't forget to include walking paths!

2. When you are satisfied with the design, add color to your park. Use colored pencils.

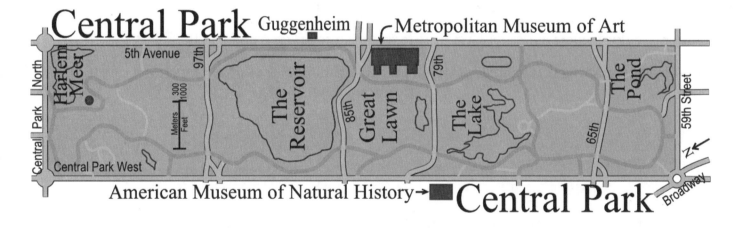

Cityscape ★☆

America is a land that has many great cities with huge skyscrapers. These skyscrapers make for a beautiful landscape. However, instead of a landscape, the view of a city's horizon line is called a **cityscape**. In this project, you will draw a cityscape looking down on the city.

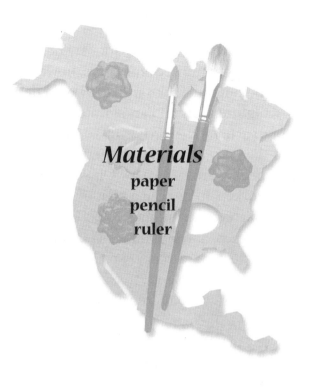

Materials
paper
pencil
ruler

1. Draw an "x" or "t" on your paper. This will be the road in your cityscape. You can draw the roads perfectly centered, as in figure 1, or you can tilt them as in figure 2. (Centered is the easiest way to go, but a more experienced artist should try the tilted version.) Making your roads wide gives the impression that the viewer is closer to the ground. Narrow roads make the buildings seem higher and the viewer farther away.

2. Place a dot in the middle of your roads where they intersect. (fig. 1) This is your vanishing point.

3. Draw a square beside the road. Use a ruler to make it straight. The square should be **parallel** to the road lines. (Parallel means it should run exactly straight with the lines.)

4. Draw lines from the three corners of the square that are closest to the vanishing point. (fig 1)

5. Erase the part of the lines that cross the road. (fig. 2) You have now completed your first skyscraper!

6. Add more skyscrapers as desired. Just be sure that each square is parallel to the roads.

7. Erase your vanishing point and any extra lines. Add details like windows, people, and cars to your picture.

Artist Profile: LOUIS SULLIVAN

Louis Sullivan is considered the father of the American skyscraper. While many architects of his era were content at copying older, European buildings, Sullivan had a different idea. He invented his own kind of building, which is now considered "Modernist" in style. Unlike most buildings of the same period, his contained very few decorations or embellishments. His work was met with varying degrees of acceptance at the time, but now he is considered visionary. His most famous building is the Wainwright Building, in St. Louis, Missouri.

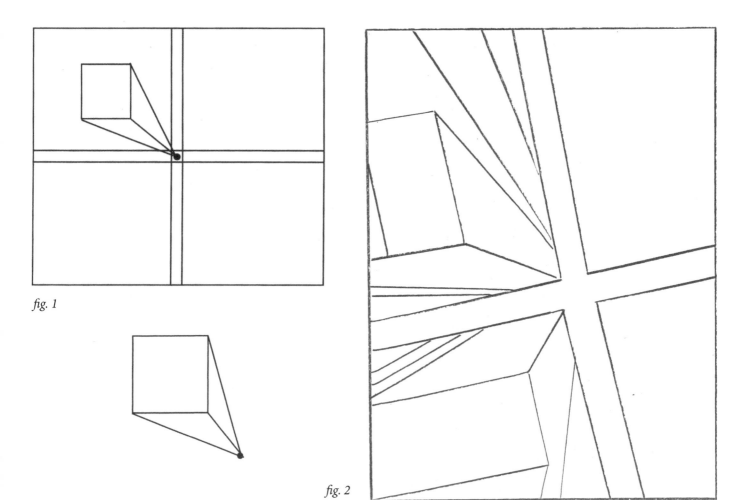

fig. 1

fig. 2

QUICKSKETCH: STATUE OF LIBERTY

Can you imagine a woman with a nose four feet long? The Statue of Liberty is that woman! She is 151 feet high and weighs 225 tons! The Statue was given to the United States as a gift from France. The sculptor, Frederic Auguste Bartholdi, got his inspiration from a tour of New York Harbor, where thousands of immigrants arrived in America after a long ocean voyage. Draw the Statue of Liberty in your geography notebook.

A sculptor would make many drawings before he begins sculpting his statue. If you were a sculptor, what kind of statue would you make? What design would best represent the country, state, or town that you live in? Draw your design beside the Statue of Liberty in your geography notebook.

Graffiti ☆

Is graffiti a form of art? There is much debate on this subject. Graffiti is considered by most to be a form of vandalism. It is always destructive and illegal to paint or deface another person's property. However, the unique and interesting variety of graffiti has led many to believe that it is a form of art. Cities in some parts of the world have dedicated special walls and areas that are legal for graffiti artists to use. Some examples of graffiti are now on display in art galleries and museums. Graffiti is traditionally done with spray paint, but for this project, we will use chalks.

Materials

paper

pencil

chalk

fixative spray

1. A tag is the signature used by someone who does graffiti. It is often a nickname or their initials. Pick a graffiti tag that represents you.

2. Use a pencil to draw your tag on the paper. Use graffiti you have seen for inspiration.

3. Fill in your design with chalks. Do not leave any blank space on the paper. (Consider using a brick or stone design for the background.)

4. Spray the graffiti with a fixative spray to seal it.

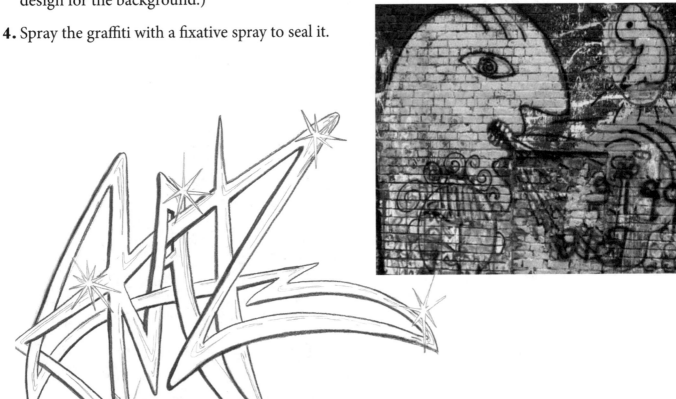

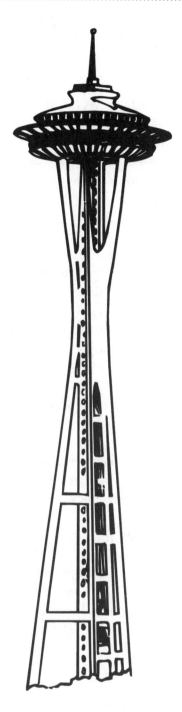

QUICKSKETCH: SEATTLE SPACE NEEDLE

The Seattle Space Needle is an interesting structure in the American northwest. It opened in 1962 for the Seattle World's Fair. It took 467 cement trucks 12 hours to pour the 5,850 tons of concrete used to make the Needle's base. The Needle is designed to withstand fierce winds and even earthquakes. There are lightning rods on top to help the Needle resist lightning damage. The Space Needle has become a symbol of Seattle and of Washington State. Draw a picture of the Space Needle in your geography notebook.

SOUTH AMERICA

Continent Summary

South America, the 4th largest continent, contains over 12 countries within its borders. Known as the "hollow continent," most of South America's population is situated on or near the coasts, leaving the central part of the continent sparsely populated. Large areas of this central part of the continent remain as natural and pristine as it was at its creation. Settlement has been hindered by the rugged Andes Mountains and nearly impenetrable Amazon forests. The Andes Mountains, near South America's western boundary, form the longest mountain system in the world. This elongated zone is prone to earthquakes and volcanic eruptions.

The Amazon is the greatest river in the world. Although the Nile in Africa is granted the title of longest in the world, the Amazon is not far behind. The Amazon is much larger by volume of water and the size of its drainage basin. It carries one fifth of the world's flowing water. Its drainage basin covers more than one third of the entire continent and is more than double that of the 2nd largest (Congo). The Amazon's depth is more than 300 feet at places near its mouth, so deep that large ocean vessels can travel inland as far as 1000 miles! The Amazon region is rich in wildlife, and there are a number of plant species there that are found nowhere else in the world. This area is diminishing in size dramatically because the forests are being logged for sugar cane plantations and cattle ranches.

The climatic zones of South America range from tropical to sub-polar zones. They grow sugar, bananas, mangoes, and rubber in the tropical north where wet and dry climates alternate. The temperate south is perfect for growing wheat, temperate fruits, and raising cattle and sheep.

Several languages are spoken here, but the main languages are Dutch, English, French, Portuguese, and Spanish. Industry includes food processing, metal and chemical industries, and textiles. There are significant mineral deposits in South America. They include tin in Bolivia, iron ore, and petroleum.

South America has a few interesting world records. The world's highest waterfall, Angel Falls (3212 feet) is in Venezuela. This is nearly three times the height of the Empire State Building. Can you imagine living where no rain has ever been recorded? There is such a place in northern Chile where the land is barren. There is not much more there than sand, rocks, borax lakes, and saline deposits. It is the Atacama Desert, one of the driest regions in the world. The southernmost city in the world is located in South America. It is on Tierra del Fuego, an island shared by Argentina and Chile. The name of this city is Ushuaia, Argentina, and it is less than 700 miles from Antarctica.

Facts
Size: 6,800,000 square miles
Rank: 4th largest continent
Highest point: Cerro Aconcagua, Argentina 22,829 ft.
Lowest Point: Salinas Chicas, Argentina -138 ft below sea level
Highest Lake: Lake Titicaca 12,506 ft.
Main rivers: Amazon
Wettest place: Quibdo, Colombia 354 inches per year
Largest country: Brazil
Smallest country: Suriname
Main languages: Dutch, English, French, Portuguese, Spanish
World's highest waterfall: Angel Falls, Venezuela 3212 ft
Industry: farming (sugar, bananas, mangoes, rubber, wheat, cattle, sheep), metal and chemical industries, food processing, textiles

South America

CARIBBEAN SEA

TRINIDAD
& TOBAGO

VENEZUELA

*Angle
Falls*

Quibdo

GUYANA

FRENCH GUIANA

COLOMBIA

SURINAME

ATLANTIC OCEAN

ECUADOR

Amazon

A
N
D
E
S

M
O
U
N
T
A
I
N
S

P E R U

B R A Z I L

Lake
Titicaca

B O L I V I A

PACIFIC OCEAN

A
n
d
e
s

M
o
u
n
t
a
i
n
s

PARAGUAY

CHILE

Tropic of Cancer

Tropic of Cancer

ATLANTIC OCEAN

A
n
d
e
s

M
o
u
n
t
a
i
n
s

A R G E N T I N A

URUGUAY

Tierra del Fuego

ad majorem Dei gloriam!

Ushuaia

S C O T I A   S E A

0

500

1000 **Miles**

GEOGRAPHY THROUGH ART   www.geomatters.com

BRAZIL 🍴

Rain Stick ☆

A rain stick is a popular craft made in Brazil and other countries in South America. Usually made from dried cactus, it mimics the sound of rain when turned up or down.

1. Decorate your tube using your poster paints or markers. A good way to draw lines around the tube is to wrap a rubber band around it and use the band as a guide. Let paint dry thoroughly.

2. Cut two pieces of construction paper slightly larger than the hole at the end of your tube. Decorate the papers. Tape one piece to the end of your tube with the packing tape.

3. Add assorted small objects to make noise, such as rice, beans, corn, or gravel. It doesn't take much to make a lot of noise.

4. Tape the other piece of paper to the other end.

5. Shake your rain stick and enjoy!

Materials
empty wrapping paper or paper towel tube
rubber bands
construction paper
scissors
clear packing tape
poster paints or markers
rice, beans, corn kernels, gravel, etc.

☆☆☆ Authentic rain sticks have cactus spines stuck inside. The pebbles hit the spines as they travel through the stick, making a truly rain-like sound. An older student, with the help of an adult, can mimic this effect by hammering nails into a sturdy cardboard mailing tube.

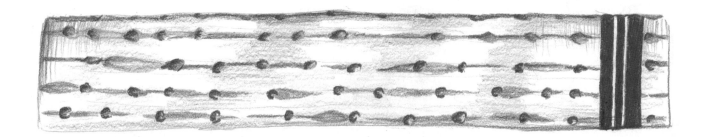

Emerald Tree Boa ☆

Snakes are a common sight in the Amazon rainforest. One example is the Emerald Tree Boa. This boa, which lives in the trees of the rainforest, is green with white stripes.

1. Cut a paper plate as shown in the diagram on this page.

2. Paint the plate to resemble an Emerald Tree Boa.

3. Punch a hole in the top of the snake. Tie a piece of string through the hole to hang your snake.

Materials
paper plate
scissors
poster or acrylic paints
paintbrushes
hole punch
string

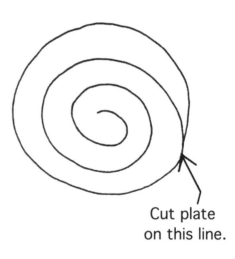

Cut plate
on this line.

Tips on Making the Color Green

The color green is a secondary color. Mix together yellow and blue and you will have green. If you add white to the green, it will be a mint green. If you put a hint of black with the green, you will get a forest green. Practice mixing greens as you make the Emerald Tree Boa.

QUICKSKETCH: FROG

The Amazon rainforest, located in Brazil and surrounding countries, is home to many different types of frogs. These frogs often have bright colors and beautiful patterns. One example is the "Blue Jeans frog." This frog, which is poisonous, has a red body with blue legs, giving it the appearance that it is wearing a pair of blue jeans. In your geography notebook, draw a frog. Color it with bright colors.

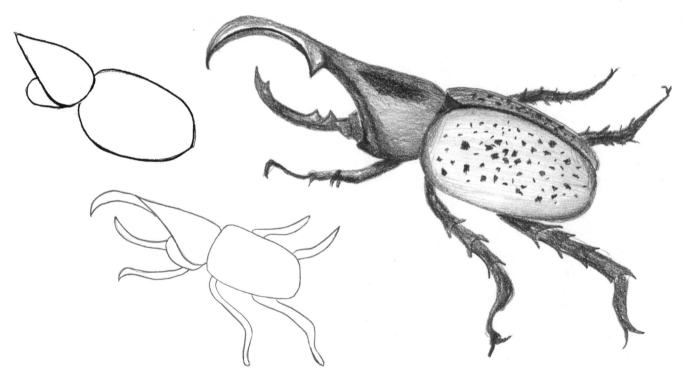

QUICKSKETCH: HERCULES BEETLE

The Hercules beetle can grow up to six inches long. It is a member of the Rhinoceros beetle family, so named because of the large horn on the head of the beetle. The Hercules beetle can carry nearly eight hundred times its own body weight! Draw a picture of this unique beetle in your geography notebook.

CHILE

Easter Island ☆

Easter Island is one of the most isolated and remote islands in the world. It is located off the coast of Chile in South America. The island is home to huge statues carved from volcanic rock. These statues, known as moai, have made Easter Island famous all over the world. For this project, you will draw the statues in one point perspective.

1. Draw a horizon line on your paper.

2. Starting where the horizon line meets the edge of the paper, draw a diagonal line to the opposite corner of the page.

3. Draw the statues between the horizon and diagonal line. The largest statues will appear closer to you, while the smaller statues will appear far away.

4. Erase the extra lines.

5. Add details and a backdrop to your picture.

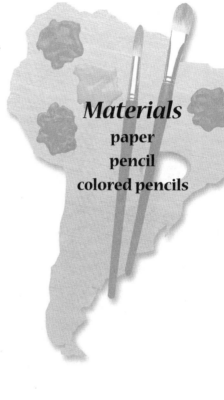

Materials
paper
pencil
colored pencils

QUICKSKETCH: HUMMINGBIRD

The Hummingbird is found in both North and South America, including the country of Chile. It is a small bird, named for the humming noise made by the bird's wings. It can hover in place at a flower by flapping its wings very rapidly. It lives on a diet of nectar from flowers, as well as the occasional insect. Draw a hummingbird in your geography notebook.

Piñata ★★☆

A piñata is a wonderful form of folk art found all over Central and South America. The piñata is used at celebrations and stuffed with candy and small toys. Children (and adults, too!) take turns hitting the piñata until it breaks open. For this project, we will make a cat-shaped piñata.

1. Inflate a large round balloon for the cat's body.

2. Mix together the flour, water, and salt. Dip the paper strips in the mixture and then place on the balloon. Each strip should overlap the next. Repeat until the balloon is completely covered. Let dry thoroughly.

3. Cut the shape of a cat's face out of a piece of construction paper. Decorate the face with markers. Glue on pipe cleaners for the whiskers.

4. Use duct or packing tape to attach the paper towel rolls to the cat for legs. For a tail, use party streamers or strips of construction paper.

5. Use poster paints to pant the body and legs of the cat.

6. Have an adult cut a hole in the top of the piñata and stuff with candy and small toys. Tape the hole shut.

7. Tape or glue on the head of the cat.

8. Hang your piñata from a tree or post. Let everyone take a turn swinging at the piñata with a bat while blindfolded. When the piñata breaks, everyone grabs as much candy as they can!

☆ For a simpler piñata, decorate a brown paper bag. Fill with candy and then staple shut. Use like a regular piñata.

QUICKSKETCH: BOMBARDIER BEETLE

The Bombardier beetle has a very interesting defense mechanism. These beetles defend themselves by spraying hot chemicals from their bodies at their attackers. The chemical is foul-tasting and creates a burning sensation.

Draw a picture in your geography notebook of a Bombardier beetle. If you are feeling inventive, try to make your own version of this beetle. You might try using modeling clay, pipe cleaners, tape, poster paint, and a small squirt gun.

ECUADOR

Tagua Nut Carvings ☆☆ ⓘ

The tagua nut comes from a species of palm tree. When left to harden in the sun, the inside turns into a hard, ivory-like substance. This has become a popular medium for sculpting in South American countries. The most common subjects are animals from the rainforests.

Materials
small white bar of soap
toothpick

1. Decide on a design for your carving. A good choice would be a South American animal.

2. Carefully carve your design using a toothpick.

⌐Culture Connection: SCRIMSHAW

Tagua nut carvings are similar to the art of scrimshaw, which we learned was practiced by sailors aboard ships during long voyages. Of course, scrimshaw was done on real animal ivory instead of tagua nut, which is sometimes called "vegetable ivory." How has geography affected these two forms of art? What does location have to do with the art someone produces? In this case, it has affected the availability of a medium. Real ivory was readily available to sailors, thus making it an excellent choice for scrimshaw. Inland South America, of course, would have little ivory. There is, however, an abundance of tagua nut, thus making it an excellent choice for carving. What things are readily available to you to create art? Look outside to see what objects might be useful for your next art project.

Butterfly Watercolors ☆

Butterflies in the rainforest come in every color of the rainbow. They also come in many different sizes, up to a foot long! For this project, we will make our own butterflies.

Materials
construction paper
pencil
scissors
water
watercolors
paintbrushes
black fine-tipped marker

1. Fold a light-colored piece of construction paper in half. Draw the outline of half a butterfly, starting at the fold. (A simple "B" shape works well.)

2. Cut along the outline of your butterfly. Unfold the paper. You should now have a butterfly shape.

3. Dip a paintbrush in a clean glass of water, then dip in the blue watercolor. Put brush back in the water. Repeat until the water is slightly tinted blue.

4. Lay your paper butterfly flat. Paint the entire surface with the blue water.

5. Before the butterfly has dried, touch three different colors of paint to the wings with your brush. Try to put the same colors in the same spots on both sides, because butterflies are usually symmetrical. Watch how the colors expand through the water!

6. Let the butterfly dry thoroughly. Add details with a black fine-tipped marker or paintbrush with black paint.

QUICKSKETCH: HARPY EAGLE

Did you know that there are over 200 species of eagles in existence? One such eagle is the Harpy Eagle. It is one of the world's largest eagles and strongest birds of prey. It can grow up to three feet tall and weigh up to twenty pounds. It survives with a diet of small mammals—including monkeys, porcupines, and the occasional small deer. When the Harpy Eagle hears a noise the feathers on her crown and around her face fan out creating a larger area to detect the sound waves. In your geography notebook, draw a Harpy Eagle.

PERU 🍴

Retablo Art ☆☆

Retablo art is a very rich tradition in Peru. This folk art is actually a box filled with tiny people arranged in various scenes to tell a story. In the past, priests carried brightly colored retablos filled with religious scenes through the mountain roads for their people to see. Now, retablos are not limited to religious stories but include local myths and legends as well.

1. With the lid on the shoebox, draw a line directly down the middle of the lid (length-wise). Cut the lid in half along this line.

2. Place the lid back on the shoebox, just like it was before you cut it. With the packing tape, tape the sides of the lid to the shoebox, only along the long side. You can now open up your retablo box.

3. Decide on what scene you want to put inside your box. Sculpt figures for your scene. Bake the figures following the clay directions.

4. While the figures are baking, paint the inside of your retablo. Paint a backdrop for the figures you have created. Be sure to paint the inside of the lid.

5. Cover the outside of your box with construction paper. Paint the outside of the box or leave it plain.

6. When the clay figures have cooled, paint them if desired. Place them in the retablo. You can secure them to the bottom using glue. After the paint and glue has thoroughly dried, you can store the retablo with the lid closed.

Materials
empty shoebox with lid
pencil
scissors
packing tape
dough clay or Sculpey
acrylic or poster paints
paintbrushes
construction paper
glue

Note: Find the recipe for dough clay in the Appendix. Sculpey, a type of clay that is baked into a plastic-like finish, would also be good for this project. It is available at your local discount or hobby store.

QuickSketch: Machu Picchu

Machu Picchu is the site of an ancient Incan city. It is located near Cuzco, Peru. Though much of the city is now in ruins, thousands of people visit every year to see this piece of history. Look at the picture on this page. Draw Machu Picchu in your geography notebook.

Macaw ☆

The macaw is a member of the parrot family. These beautiful birds are native to South America, but are kept as pets all over the world. There are many species, each with a different vibrant color. These social birds can live up to sixty years. They often mimic the sounds they hear, including human voices.

Materials
heavy paper
pencil
oil pastels

1. Look at the woodburning picture of the macaws below. It might also help to look in a book or on the Internet at color pictures of this bird.

2. Lightly sketch a picture of the bird on a heavy piece of paper.

3. Color your picture with bright colors using oil pastels. With oil pastels, you can put many layers of color. Try this as you color your drawing.

Woodburning by Kathy Wright

QUICKSKETCH: LLAMA

A very common animal in Peru is the llama. Perhaps because of that, it is often seen in Peruvian art. A llama is a member of the camel family. It is primarily used in South America as a pack animal, moving supplies and goods. Its coat is also used to make yarn. A llama can grow to be up to six feet tall and five hundred pounds. In your geography notebook, draw a picture of a llama.

Bulls of Pucara ☆☆

A popular theme in Peruvian folk art is the bull. Especially famous are the clay bulls made in the city of Pucara and in other cities around the Lake Titicaca region. These clay bulls are often decorated with bright floral designs.

1. Shape a light color of modeling clay into a bull shape. Use the bulls on this page for reference.

2. Add details, such as eyes, to your bull using the toothpicks.

3. Dry your clay according to the directions of the manufacturer.

4. Paint a floral design on your bull.

Materials
modeling clay
toothpicks
poster paints
paintbrushes

APPENDIX

Recipes and Templates

Outline Maps

CLAY RECIPES

Basic Land Clay

This clay is perfect for making land formations, maybe to go with your castle, log cabin, or other model.

2 cups salt
2 cups flour
1 1/3 cups water

Combine ingredients. Stir well.
Place on cardboard and make land formations (mountains, hills, etc.).

Sawdust Clay

4-5 cups sawdust
1-cup wheat paste
1/4 cup salt

Mix with water until a clay-like consistency is achieved.
Air dry or bake at 275°F until clay has hardened, about one hour. (It really depends on the size of the piece you are making.)
Note: Wheat paste can be purchased at your local hardware store.

Coffee clay

This recipe comes from Robbie Blum in Denver, Colorado. It makes bricks that look like real stone!

1 cup flour
1/2 cup salt
1 cup used coffee grinds
1/2 cup cold, leftover coffee

Combine ingredients in a bowl until well-blended.
Knead on a floured surface until smooth.
Air dry or bake at 175°F for 30 minutes.

Dough clay

This clay is perfect for making jewelry, magnets, or other small designs.

4 tablespoons flour
1 tablespoon salt
2 tablespoons water

Combine ingredients.
Knead until smooth.
Air dry or bake at 350°F for one hour.

Edible clay

Here is an easy-to-make clay that tastes good, too.

1 cup smooth peanut butter
1 1/3 cups powdered milk
3 tablespoons honey

Mix in a bowl until smooth.
Sculpt and eat!

Play dough

Play dough cracks as it dries, so it is not good for making projects to save. However, it is a great clay to use with small children who just want to play.

1 cup flour
1/2 cup salt
2 teaspoons cream of tartar
1 cup water
1 teaspoon vegetable oil
food coloring

Stir together ingredients, adding drops of food coloring until desired color is reached.
Cook mixture over medium heat for two to three minutes.
Knead into a ball. Store in airtight container.

ILLUSTRATED GEOGRAPHY TERMS

Piedmont
An area of rolling land along the foot of a mountain.

Plateau
A large level or nearly level area of elevated land.

Sandbar
A long narrow bank of sand in a body of water.

Dock
The water or space between two wharves; sometimes used to refer to the wharves themselves.

Elevation
Height or distance above sea level.

Reservoir
A natural or artifical lake usually made by damming a stream of running water.

GEOGRAPHY THROUGH ART

ILLUSTRATED GEOGRAPHY TERMS

Counry *Peoples' Republic of China*

Continent *Asia*

Facts

Area *705,407 sq. miles*

Population *1,321,851,888*

Capital *Beijing*

Government *Communist Party-led state*

Language *Mandarin Chinese*

Currency *Yuan Renminbi (CNY)*

Chief Cities *Bejing (capital), Shanghi, Guangdong, Shenzhen, Tianjin, & Wuhan*

Rivers & Other Bodies of Water *Yellow River, Yangtze River, Xi River*

Natural Resources *coal, iron ore, oil, natural gas, mercury, tin, tungsten, antimony, aluminum, & hydropower*

Products *iron, steel, coal, machine bulding, armaments, textiles & apparel, oil, cement, & chemical fertilizers*

Interesting Information

The highest point in the world is at Mt. Everest located in the Himalayas.

During the Han Dynasty (221-206bc) paper and the seismograph were invented, steel was first made, and Buddhism was first introduced.

The Great Wall of China extends about 1500 miles and can be seen from space. It is 15-25 feet thick and was built in the 3rd century.

Description of Land & Climate

China is divided into three regions.

In the <u>Western region</u> sits the mountainous plateau of Tibet which is the highest region in the world with its Himalayan Mountains.

The <u>Northern Region</u> includes the Gobi and Taklemaken deserts.

The low-lying <u>Eastern Region</u> includes the coastline.

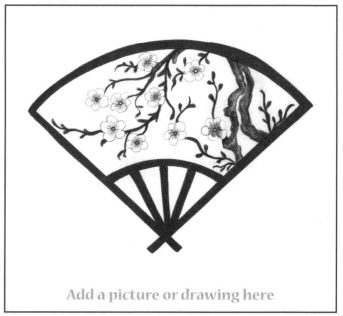

Add a picture or drawing here

GEOGRAPHY THROUGH ART

Counry _____

Continent _____

Facts

Area _____

Population _____

Capital _____

Government _____

Language _____

Currency _____

Chief Cities _____

_____

Rivers & Other Bodies of Water _____

_____

Natural Resources _____

_____

_____

Products _____

_____

_____

Interesting Information

Flag

Description of Land & Climate

Add a picture or drawing here

Chinese Paper Cutting Designs

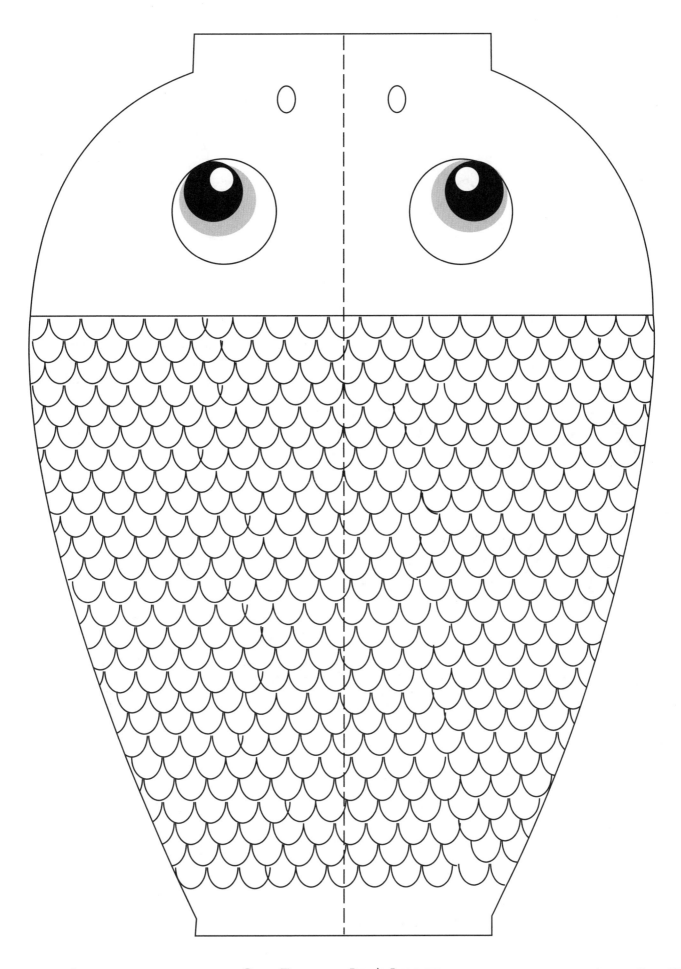

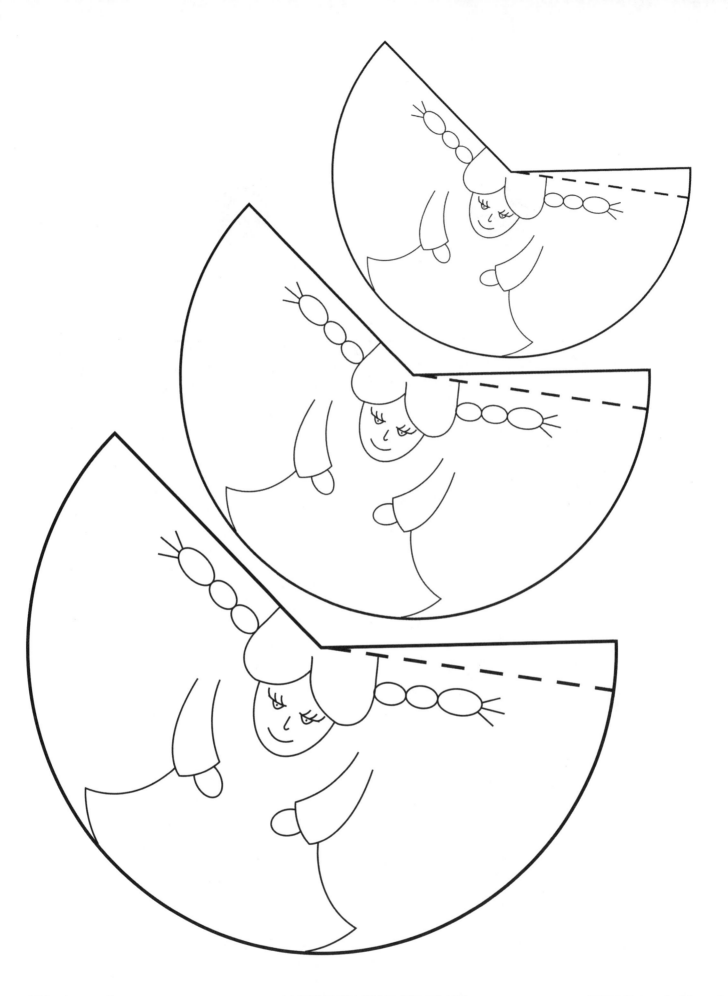

MATRYOSKA DOLL TEMPLATE

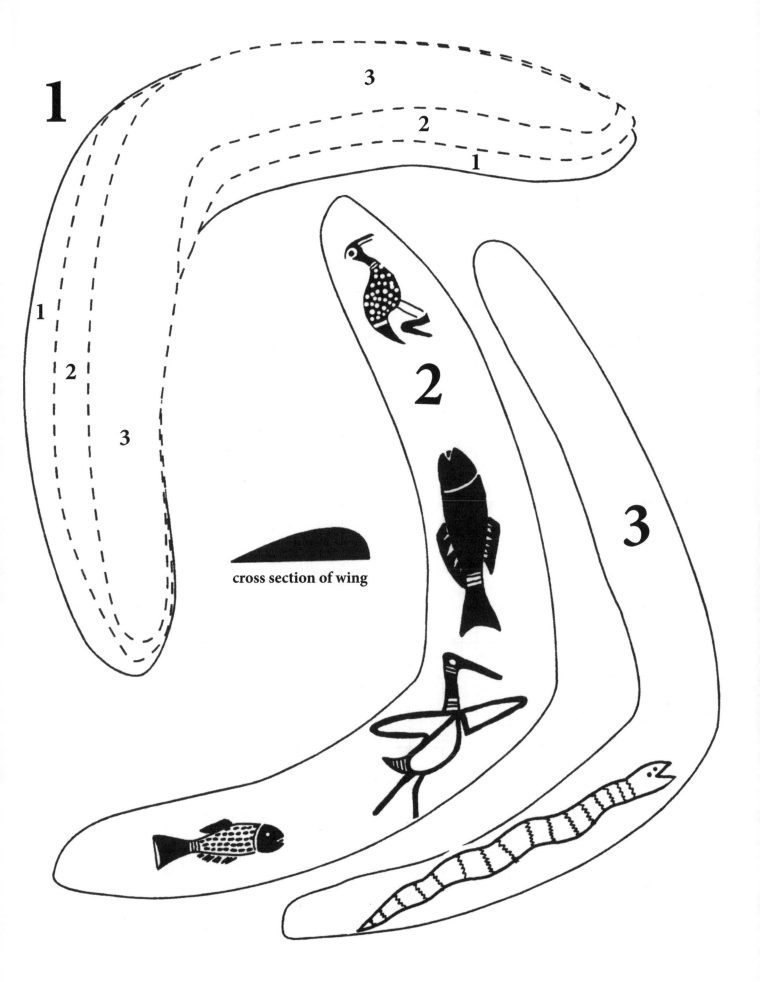

cross section of wing

GRAPH PAPER GRID

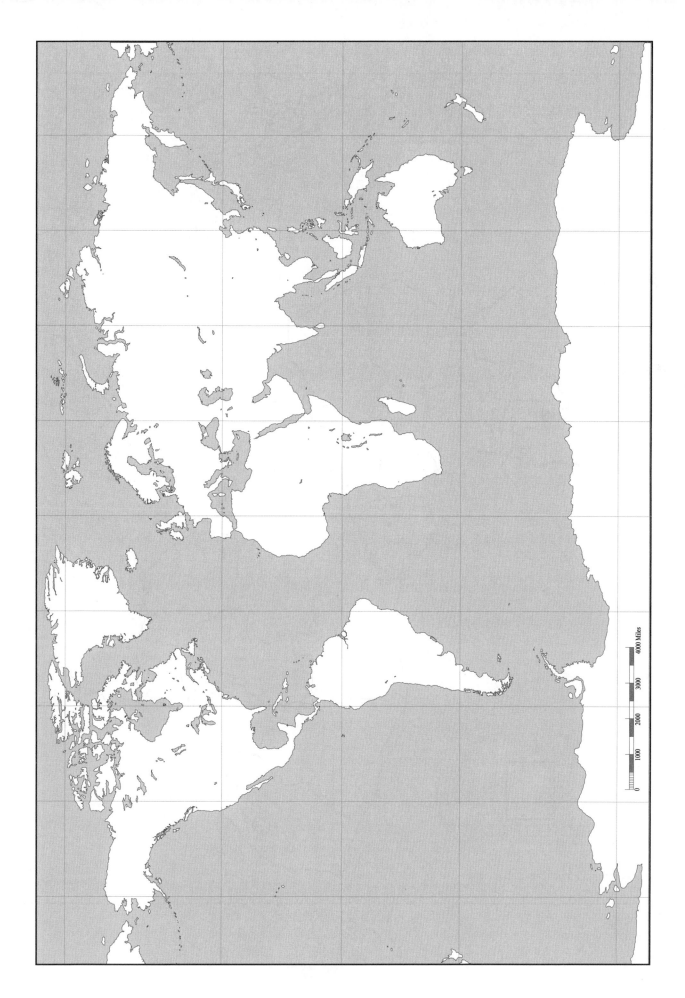

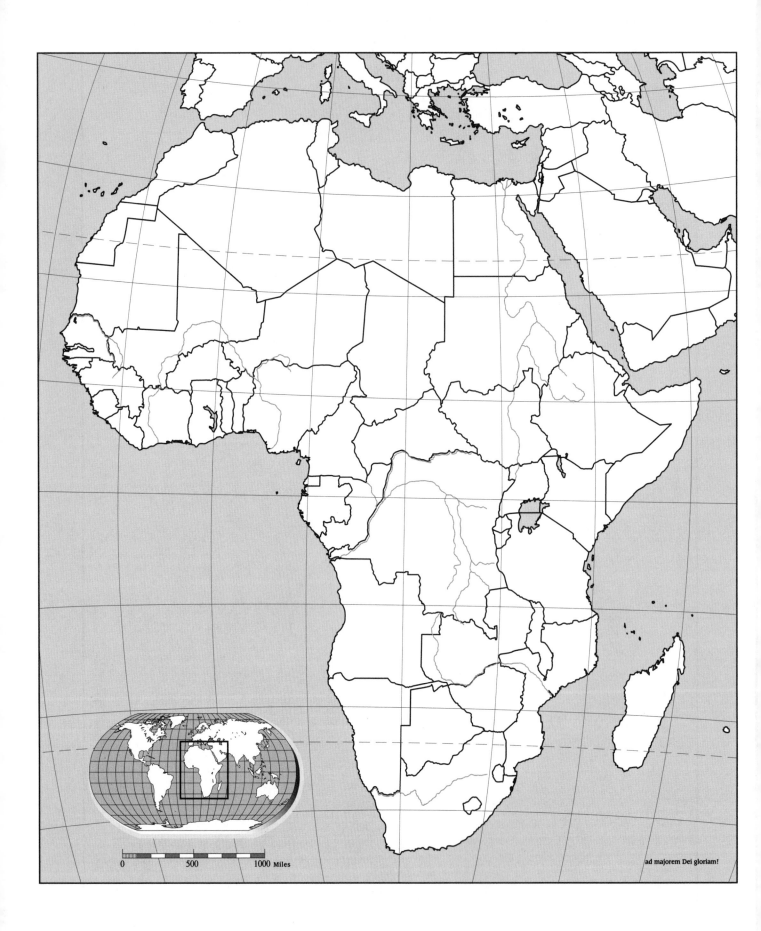

ad majorem Dei gloriam!

AFRICA

0   500   1000 Miles

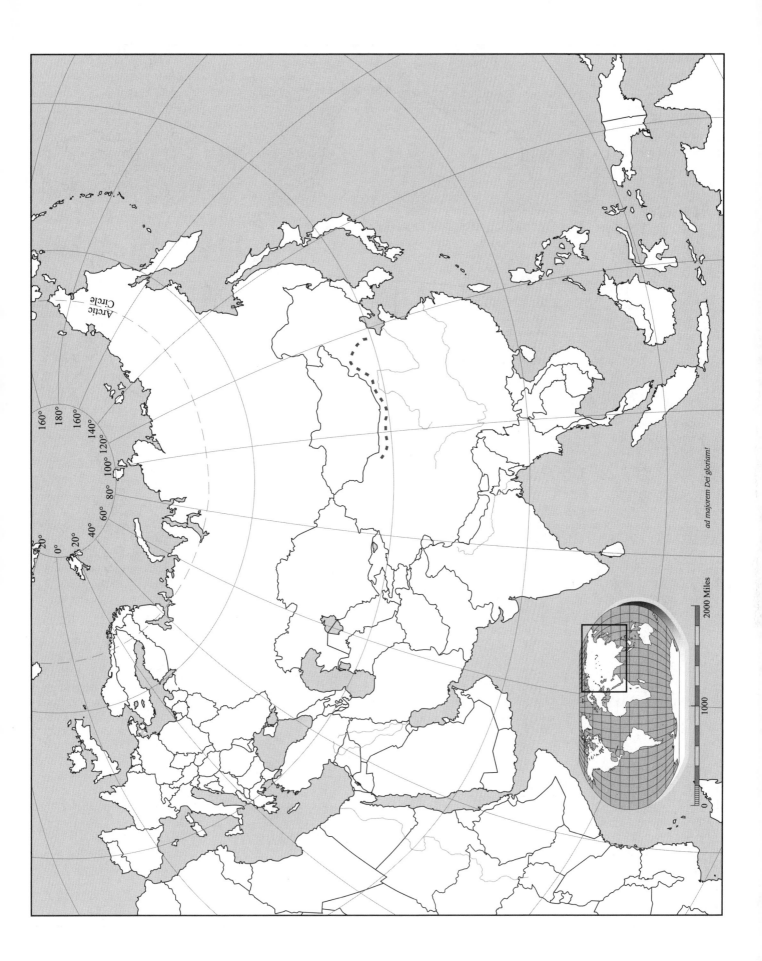

Arctic Circle

160° 180° 160° 140° 120° 100° 80° 60° 40° 20° 0° 20°

ad majorem Dei gloriam!

2000 Miles

1000

0

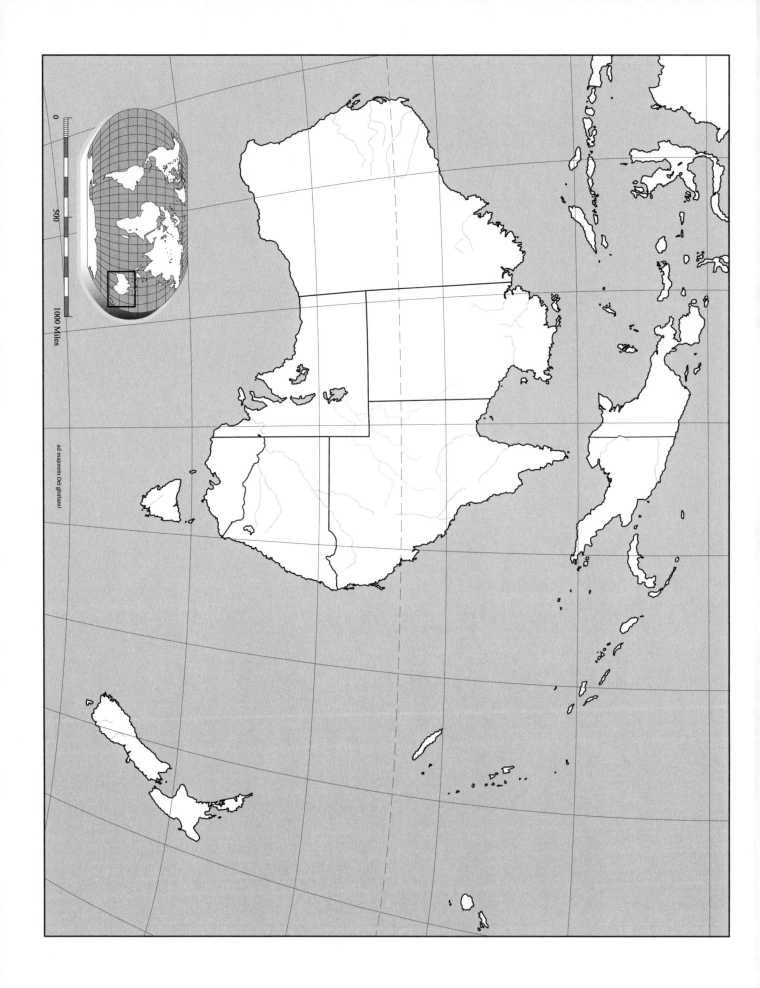

AUSTRALIA

ad majorem Dei gloriam!

0

500

1000 Miles

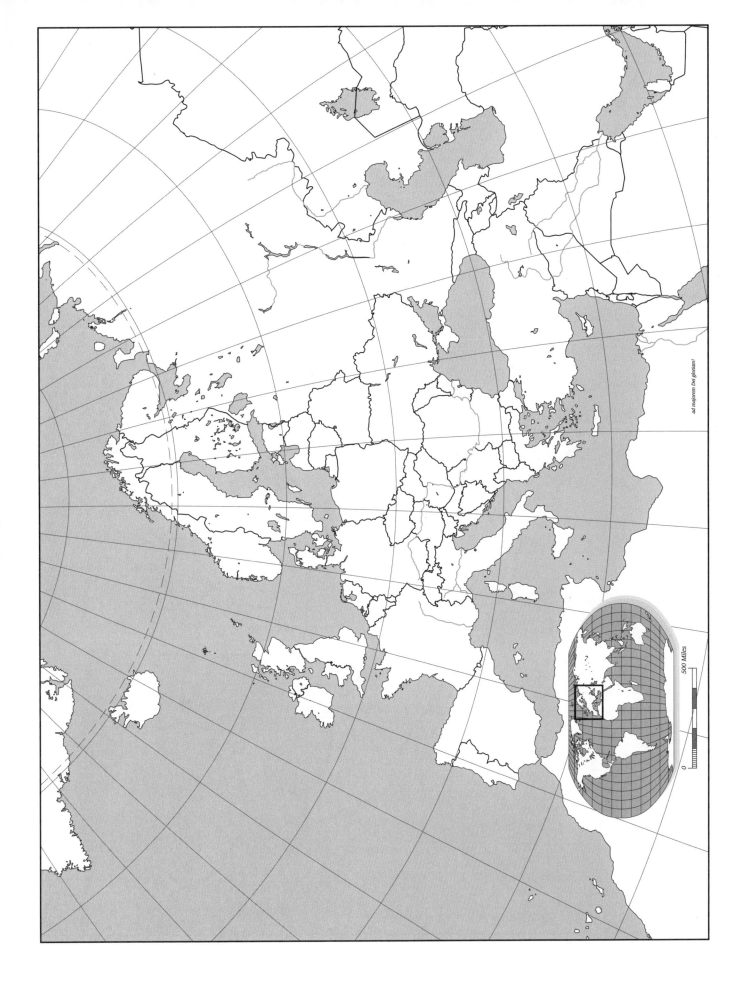

ad majorem Dei gloriam!

500 Miles

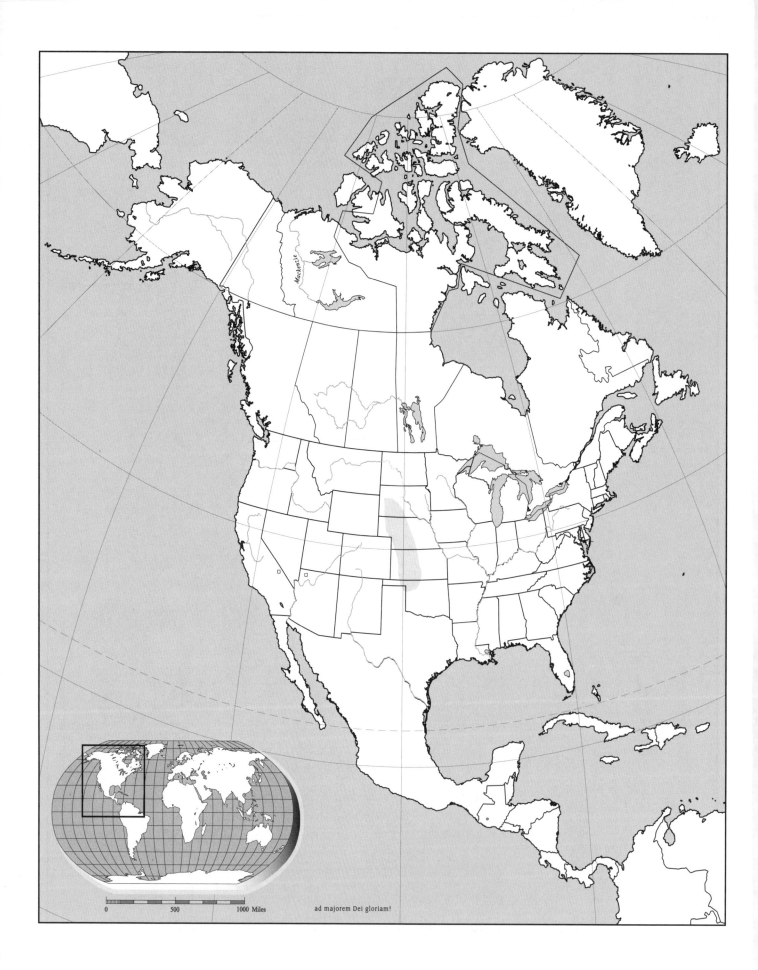

Mackenzie

0   500   1000 Miles

ad majorem Dei gloriam!

NORTH AMERICA

Angle
Falls

ad majorem Dei gloriam!

0   500   1000 Miles

GLOSSARY

Art Terms

Assemblage - creating art by putting together found objects

Batik - a piece of fabric which has been dyed on top of wax designs

Caricature - a quick sketch drawn for fun that exaggerates a person's most noticeable features

Cartography - the art and science of making maps

Cartouche - used in hieroglyphics, the oval in which the names of royalty were inscribed

Cityscape - the view of a city's horizon line

Collage - a picture put together from many different parts

Fresco - a painting done in wet plaster

Gyotaku - Japanese fish printing

Hieroglyphics - the symbolic written language of the ancient Egyptians

Horizon line - the line in a piece of art where the sky meets the ground

Megalithic structure - an arrangement of huge stones that shows little evidence of having been carved or sculpted

Negative space - the background space of the art

One dimensional - flat, an object without height, width, or depth

Orthogonal - the diagonal lines in a sketch that are drawn from the vanishing point to the object

Orthostat - a large rock that has been placed in a vertical position

Paper mache - the art of making objects around different forms using strips of paper dipped in a glue paste

Parallel lines - lines that run alongside each other

Pictographs - a word that actually looks like what it is

Positive space - the part of the art containing the subject matter, as opposed to the background or negative space

Profile - a portrait of a person done using the side view

Realistic - a piece of art that looks very similar to the actual thing being portrayed

Runes - letters of the Viking alphabet

Seals - Chinese identifying marks placed in the body of the art

Sumi-e - the Japanese art of painting pictures with ink in as few strokes as possible

Storyboard - one of the first steps in movie making; the drawings that correlate to scenes in the movie

Stylized - a piece of art that is a fanciful, unrealistic version of what is being portrayed

Symmetry - when something is identical on both sides

Tangram Puzzle - an ancient Chinese puzzle consisting of seven shapes which must be formed into a picture

Three dimensional - an object that has height, width, and depth

Topography - the study of the way the land lays

Two-point perspective - a drawing done with two vanishing points

Vanishing point - the point on the horizon line at which visibility ends

Wycinanki - the Polish folk art of paper cutting

Geography Terms

Archipelago – a broad area of water containing several islands

Canal – a channel constructed for navigation, irrigation or drainage

Channel – a narrow strip of water, usually the best passage for ships because of its depth

Coastline – land bordering the sea

Continent –any one of the seven largest bodies of land on the earth's surface: Australia, Asia, Africa, Antarctica, Europe, North America, and South America

Desert – a dry, barren region

Fjord – a deep, narrow inlet of the sea between high, steep banks

Inland – pertaining to the interior of a country

Isthmus - a narrow piece of land that joins two larger bodies of land or joins a peninsula with the mainland

Lake – large inland body of water

Land – the part of the earth's surface above the level of the sea or ocean

Mountain – a lofty elevation on the earth's surface

Oceania – the collective name for the lands of the Pacific Ocean, especially of the central and South Pacific. It includes Micronesia, Melanesia, and Polynesia and sometimes Australia, New Zealand and the Malay Archipelago.

Plateau – a large level area of elevated land

River – a relatively large natural stream of water, usually fed by another body of water

Sea – a large body of water partly or nearly surrounded by land

Sea level - the average level of the surface of the water as measured on the shoreline

Shore – land bordering a lake, sea, or large river

Volcano – a cone-shaped mountain formed by lava and cinders that erupted through a crater; an opening in the earth's surface from which flows or has flowed molten rock, steam, cinders, gas and rock fragments

INDEX

Index

One Week
ART IMMERSION

visualmanna.com

Sharon Jeffus has developed an advanced fine art and graphic art program for high school students and church groups to learn excellence in the visual arts. She also has two dual credit AP art classes available that can be taken through Visual Manna Academy Art School. Email her at visualmanna@gmail.com or go to visualmanna.com for more information. Her art through the core books are available at rainbowresources.com. You can check out her free video lessons available at: http://ourhomeschoolforum.com/videos/interactive-lessons/art-through-the-year-with-sharon-jeffus-lesson-1-post-impressionism-and-line/

Adventures of Munford Series
by Jamie Aramini

Although he's just two parts hydrogen and one part oxygen, Munford is all adventure. He can be rain, snow, sleet, or steam. He has traveled the world in search of excitement. Throughout history, he has been present at some of the most important and world-changing events.

Fun and educational, Munford will inspire your children to learn more about many of history's greatest events. These readers make a great addition to your learning experience in areas such as history, geography, and science. This book series was written on an elementary reading level, but provides plenty of read-aloud entertainment for the entire family! Paperback, $8.95.

The American Revolution

In this adventure, Munford travels to colonial America and experiences first–hand the events leading to the American Revolution. He meets famed American Founding Fathers, such as Samuel Adams, Thomas Jefferson, and George Washington. He joins the Sons of Liberty under cover of night to dump tea into Boston Harbor. He tags along for Paul Revere's most famous ride, and even becomes a part of the Declaration of Independence in a way that you might not expect!

The Klondike Gold Rush

In this adventure, Munford finds himself slap into the middle of the Klondike Gold Rush. He catches gold fever on this dangerous, yet thrilling, adventure. Meet some of the Gold Rush's most famous characters, like gold baron Alex McDonald or the tricky villain named Soapy Smith. Take a ride on the Whitehorse Rapids, and help Munford as he pans for gold. This is an adventure you won't soon forget!

Munford Meets Lewis & Clark

Join Munford on an epic adventure with Meriwether Lewis and William Clark, as they make their perilous journey in search of the Northwest Passage to the Pacific Ocean.

Munford Meets Robert Fulton

Join Munford— the world's most daring water molecule in his latest adventure! Munford joins forces with Robert Fulton, inventor of the world's first practical steam boat!

Eat Your Way Through the USA
by Loreé Pettit

Taste your way around the U.S.A. without leaving your own dining room table! Each state has its unique geographical features, culinary specialities, and agricultural products. These influence both the ingredients that go into a recipe and the way food is prepared. Compliment your geography lesson and tantalize your tastebuds at the same time with this outstanding cookbook.

This cookbook includes a full meal of easy to follow recipes from each state. Though they aren't written at a child's level, it's easy to include your students in the preparation of these dishes. Cooking together provides life skills and is a source of bonding and pride. More than just a cookbook, it is a taste buds-on approach to geography. Spiral bound, 118 pages, $14.95

Eat Your Way Around the World
by Jamie Aramini

Get out the sombrero for your Mexican fiesta! Chinese egg rolls… corn pancakes from Venezuela… fried plantains from Nigeria. All this, and more, is yours when you take your family on a whirlwind tour of over thirty countries in this unique international cookbook. Includes a full meal of recipes from each country. Recipes are easy to follow, and ingredients are readily available. Jam-packed with delicious dinners, divine drinks, and delectable desserts, this book is sure to please.

The entire family will be fascinated with tidbits of culture provided for each country including: Etiquette Hints, Food Profiles, and Culture a la Carté. For more zest, add an activity and violà, create a memorable learning experience that will last for years to come. Some activities include: Food Journal, Passport, and World Travel Night. Spiral bound, 120 pages, $14.95

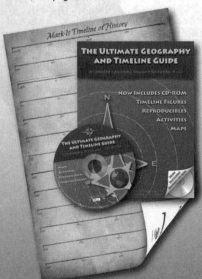

The Ultimate Geography and Timeline Guide
by Maggie Hogan and Cindy Wiggers

Grades K - 12

Learn how to construct timelines, establish student notebooks, teach geography through literature, and integrate science with activities on volcanoes, archaeology, and other subjects. Use the complete multi-level geography course for middle and high school students. Now includes CD-ROM of all reproducible activity and planning pages. Use for all students kindergarden through high school. Paperback with CD-ROM, 353 pages, $39.95

- 18 Reproducible Outline Maps
- Teaching Tips
- Planning Charts
- Over 150 Reproducible Pages
- Over 300 Timeline Figures
- Lesson Plans
- Scope and Sequence
- Flash Cards
- Games

Mark-It Timeline of History

There's hardly no better way to keep history in perspective than creating a timeline in tandem with your history studies. This poster is just the tool to do so. Write or draw images of events as they are studied, or attach timeline figures to aid student understanding and comprehension of the topic at hand. 23" x 34". Laminated, $10.95, Paper (folded), $5.95

Lewis & Clark - Hands On

Art and English Activities

by Sharon Jeffus

Follow the experiences of Meriwether Lewis and William Clark with hands-on art and writing projects associated with journal entries made during the Corps of Discovery Expedition. Ideal for adding interest to any Lewis and Clark study or to teach drawing and journaling. Includes profiles of American artists, step by step drawing instructions, actual journal entries, and background information about this famous adventure.
Paperback, 80 pages, $12.95

Profiles from History

by Ashley (Strayer) Wiggers

When studying history, a human connection is the most important connection that we can make. In *Profiles from History*, your student will not only learn about twenty famous people – but also why each one is worthy of remembrance. Everyone knows that Benjamin Franklin was a great inventor, but how many realize he was also a great man? He valued helping people more than making money or becoming famous. He refused to patent his popular Franklin stove, so more families could keep their homes warm during the cold, winter months. *Profiles from History* tells stories like this one, stories of greatness and inspiration. Each profile includes fun activities such as crosswords, word search, & timeline usage. Paperback, $16.95

Also Available:
Profiles from History - Volume 2   Profiles from History - Volume 3

Geography Through Art

by Sharon Jeffus and Jamie Aramini

Geography Through Art is the ultimate book of international art projects. Join your children on an artistic journey to more than twenty-five countries spanning six continents (includes over a dozen United States projects). Previously published by Visual Manna as *Teaching Geography Through Art*, Geography Matters has added a number of enhancements and practical changes to this fascinating art book. Use this book as an exciting way to supplement any study of geography, history, or social studies. You'll find yourself reaching for this indispensable guide again and again to delight and engage students in learning about geography through the culture and art of peoples around the world.
Paperback, 190 pages, $19.95

Timeline Figures on CD-ROM

Kids love the look of their timelines when they add color and variety. Students can draw on their timeline, write events and dates, and add timeline figures. We've created two different sets of color timeline figures that are ready to print from any computer. There are over 350 figures in each set plus templates to create your own. Our figures are appealing in style, simple to use, and include color-coding and icons to aid memory. Available with biblical events and general world events. CD-ROM (Mac & Windows Compatible), $19.95

- Reproducible Outline Maps -

Reproducible outline maps have a myriad of uses in the home, school, and office. Uncle Josh's quality digital maps provide opportunities for creative learning at all ages. His maps feature rivers and grid lines where possible, and countries are shown in context with their surroundings. (No map of Germany "floating" in the center of the page, here!) When students use outline maps and see the places they are studying in context they gain a deeper understanding of the subject at hand.

Uncle Josh's Outline Map Book

Take advantage of those spontaneous teaching moments when you have this set of outline maps handy. They are:

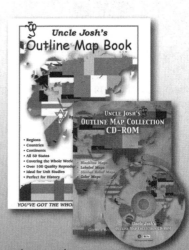

• Over 100 reproducible maps
• 15 world regions
• Continents with and without borders
• 25 countries
• Each of the 50 United States
• 8 U.S. regions

Useful for all grades and topics, this is by far one of the best book of reproducible outline maps you'll find. Paperback, 128 pages, $19.95

Uncle Josh's Outline Map Collection CD-ROM

In addition to all maps in *Uncle Josh's Outline Map Book* the CD-Rom includes color, shaded-relief, and labeled maps. Over 260 printable maps plus bonus activities. CD-ROM (Mac & Windows), $26.95

- Large-scale Maps -

Large-scale maps are great for detail labeling and for family or classroom use. Laminated Mark-It maps can be reused for a variety of lessons. Quality digital map art is used for each of the map titles published and laminated by Geography Matters. Choose from large scale continents, regions, United States, and world maps. US and World available in both outline version and with state, country, and capitals labeled. Ask about our ever expanding library of full, color shaded-relief maps. Paper and laminated, each title available separately or in discounted sets.

Trail Guide to Geography Series -
by Cindy Wiggers

The *Trail Guide to Geography* series is a multi-level geography curriculum guide for elementary grades through High School. Three books in the *Trail Guide to ...Geography* series include U.S., World, and Bible geography. Each book provides clear directions and assignment choices to encourage self-directed learning as students create their own personal geography notebooks. Daily atlas drills, mapping activities, and various weekly assignment choices address learning styles in a way that has kids asking for more!

Trail Guide features:
- Weekly lesson plans – for 36 weeks
- 5-minute daily atlas drills (2 questions/day, four days/week)
- 3 levels of difficulty – all ages participate together
- Weekly mapping assignments
- A variety of weekly research and hands-on activity choices

Student Notebooks are available on CD-ROM

Trail Guide Levels
The *Trail Guide* Levels are just a guide. Select a level according to student ability, and match level with the appropriate atlas or student notebook.

- Primary: grades 2–4
- Intermediate: grades 5–7
- Secondary: grades 8–12

All 3 levels in each book!

Note: Primary is ideal for independent 4th graders. Second and third graders will need plenty of guidance. If your oldest is 2nd–3rd grade range, please consider *Galloping the Globe* or *Cantering the Country* first.

Trail Guide to U.S. Geography
Grades 2 - 12

"The *Trail Guide to U.S. Geography* provides lots of guidance while allowing for (and encouraging) flexibility and this is just the balance most homeschool moms need! The manual is easy to navigate and I am very impressed with how thoroughly material is covered. This resource is destined to be a favorite with homeschool families for years to come!"
–Cindy Prechtel, homeschoolingfromtheheart.com
Paperback, 144 pages, $18.95

Trail Guide to World Geography
Grades 2 - 12

"We have the *Trail Guide to World Geography* and **love** it!! We are using it again this year just for the questions... I will never sell this guide!! I am looking forward to doing the U.S. one next year."
–Shannon, OK
Paperback, 128 pages, $18.95

Trail Guide to Bible Geography
Grades 2 - 12

"Here is another winner from Geography Matters! *Trail Guide to Bible Geography* is multi-faceted, user-friendly, and suited to a wide range of ages and abilities."
–Jean Hall, Eclectic Homeschool Association
Paperback, 128 pages, $18.95

Galloping the Globe
Grades K - 4
by Loreé Pettit and Dari Mullins

"If you've got kindergarten through fourth grade students, and are looking for unit study material for geography, hold on to your hat and get ready for *Galloping the Globe!* Loreé Pettit and Dari Mullins have written this great resource to introduce children to the continents and some of their countries. This book is designed to be completed in one to three years, depending on how much time you spend on each topic. And for each continent, there are suggestions and topics galore." –Leslie Wyatt, www.homeschoolenrichment.com

Organized by continent, incorporates student notebooking, and covers these topics:
- Basic Geography
- History and Biographies
- Literature
- Science
- Bible
- Activities
- Internet Sources
- Language Arts

The 2010 edition of *Galloping the Globe* includes an Activity CD-ROM jam-packed with all the reproducible activity sheets found in the book plus added bonus pages. Paperback with CD-ROM, 272 pages, $29.95

Cantering the Country
Grades 1–5
by Loreé Pettit and Dari Mullins

Saddle up your horses and strap on your thinking caps. Learning geography is an adventure. From the authors who brought you *Galloping the Globe,* you'll love its U.S. counterpart, *Cantering the Country.* This unit study teaches a wide range of academic and spiritual disciplines using the geography of the U.S. as a starting point. With this course, you won't have to put aside one subject to make time for another. They're all connected! This comprehensive unit study takes up to three years to complete and includes all subjects except math and spelling. Incorporates student notebooking and covers these topics:

- U.S. Geography
- Character
- Science
- Language Arts
- Activities
- Literature
- Civics
- History and Biographies
- Internet Sources

In addition to the 250+ page book, you will receive a CD-ROM packed full of reproducible outline maps and activities. Dust off your atlas and get ready to explore America! Paperback with CD-ROM, 272 pages, $29.95